MICROECONOMIC ISSUES TODAY

MICROECONOMIC ISSUES TODAY

Alternative Approaches

Sixth Edition

Robert B. Carson
Wade L. Thomas
and Jason Hecht

M.E. Sharpe
Armonk, New York
London, England

Library of Congress Cataloging-in-Publication Data

Carson, Robert Barry, 1934–
Microeconomic issues today : alternative approaches / Robert B. Carson,
Wade L. Thomas, and Jason Hecht. — 6th ed.
p.   cm.
Includes bibliographical references and index.
ISBN 0-7656-0364-0 (pbk. : alk. paper)
1. Microeconomics. 2. United States—Economic conditions—1981–
I. Thomas, Wade L.   II. Hecht, Jason, 1958–   .   III. Title.
HB172.C373   1999
338.5′0973—dc21   98-29533
CIP

Printed in the United States of America

The paper used in this publication meets the minimum requirements of
American National Standard for Information Sciences—
Permanence of Paper for Printed Library Materials,
ANSI Z 39.48-1984.

BM (p)   10   9   8   7   6   5   4   3   2

Contents

List of Figures and Tables

Figures

Tables

Preface To
Economic Issues Today

Right at the outset, the senior author (you know, as in "senior citizen") offers his apologies to longtime friends and adopters of _Economic Issues Today_. A considerable time, indeed, has passed since the book has been revised and updated, and many of you have been inconvenienced by its virtual unavailability for the last couple of years. This state of affairs commenced with the decision of its original publisher (St. Martin's Press) to discontinue its college economics list and was compounded by the fact that the senior and then sole author retired from the State University of New York. One of the fascinating things that one discovers about retirement is that there simply isn't time to do anything. That sounds like—and perhaps it is—a lame excuse. In any case, those of you who helped introduce _Economic Issues Today_ and its split versions to over a quarter of a million young readers or who, perhaps, encountered it as an undergraduate, deserved better, and for this the senior editor is deeply regretful.

Of course, those familiar with past editions of _Economic Issues Today_ will note the addition of two new authors for the current effort, Wade L. Thomas and Jason Hecht. The senior author welcomes his two younger colleagues and friends to this venture and is certain their important efforts in keeping this book up to date, relevant, and available will be readily evident. All three of us welcome any suggestions that will improve the content and coverage of _Economic Issues Today_ and its usefulness for those beginning their study of economics.

As should be expected, the current edition reflects considerable updating and revision in its Introduction and fourteen Issues. Three of the Issues—"Financing Government," "Welfare Reform,"and "Inflation"—are brand new. Four others—"Growth and Stability," "Unemployment," "International Economics," and "The Market Versus Planning and Control"—have been extensively rewritten. All other issues have been edited closely so as to bring data and arguments up to date.

Two decades have passed since the publication of the first edition of _Economic Issues Today_ (and its macroeconomic and microeconomic split versions). Needless to say, a lot of "economic water" has gone over the dam since 1978. Accordingly, the content of *Economic Issues Today* has undergone many changes through this, its sixth edition. Yet, the underlying philosophy and pedagogical objectives of the book remain the same: to introduce those uninitiated in the ways of economists to the breadth and richness of economic reasoning.

The book continues to require no background in the methods of economic analysis, and as much as posssible it avoids the use of economic jargon in favor of everyday language. This edition of *Economic Issues Today*, like previous ones, stresses the ideological choices that exist in economic thought and that often cause ordinary citizens to be confused about what economists *do* and what economists *believe*. As ever, it is meant to be a provocative book, more concerned with provoking discussion and thought than in presenting "right" solutions to problems. It remains committed to the belief that real economic solutions are possible in a democratic society only when all alternatives are known and considered.

Although longtime users are familiar with the text's philosophy and perspectives, new readers might benefit from an explanation of why the authors undertook this project in the first place and how, in fact, the book is organized.

All too frequently, students begin their study of economics with the impression that economists are bland and monolithic when discussing important issues confronting the general society. We may as well admit that the profession sometimes exhibits a tendency to blandness in its public utterances, but surely any supposed unanimity toward social policy questions has vanished. With the rise of an influential Radical caucus within the discipline, beginning in the late 1960s, and the more recent resurgence of variations of laissez-faire ideology, any facade of consensus has clearly been broken down. The application of economic theory to issues of public policy more and more reflects a range of choice from Conservative to Liberal to Radical.

For the student struggling with basic theory and analytic tools, as well as for the ordinary citizen overwhelmed by economic data in the newspapers and on the TV evening news, it is hard to avoid confusion over what economists really think about the problems facing the nation. This book begins with the assumption that the answers economists give to policy questions can be usefully compared and analyzed according to the particular biases of their arguments and the probable outcomes of their proposals. In other words, differences in economic logic and interpretation of evidence are not so much a function of skill mastery as they are the expression of strongly held social and political opinions. The text also assumes that economics as a body of knowledge takes on greater meaning and is more readily comprehended when it is viewed in this way.

For each issue, a Conservative, Liberal, and Radical analysis and proposed solution are presented in turn as the valid approach to the problem. On one page, there may be a vigorous and unyielding defense of laissez-faire and the market economy; on another, a program for the elimination or modification of the free market. This is not the way economic analysis and theory are usually taught, but it is what the practice of economics is about. In the real world, the citizen and the economist make public policy choices that protect, attack, or modify the market mechanism. We may defend our positions in terms of economic logic, but behind our proofs lies our political and ideological view of the world. This book attempts to examine the relationship between ideological values and the economic theories and policies that are their outcome.

Since the text presents a wide range of prespectives on a number of currently sensitive issues, it should provoke disagreement, controversy, and discussion. In itself, the book does not urge a particular ideological position or a particular variety of economic analysis. The decision to select or reject this or that point of view is left—as it should be—to the reader.

Each chapter is self-contained and may be assigned in any order the instructor chooses. There are relatively few footnotes or direct references to specific economists, although the ideas of many contemporary economists and schools of economic thought will be apparent. The bibliography at the end is offered for anyone wishing to dig a little more deeply into an issue or a particular economic perspective or approach.

The senior author would like to thank Michael Weber, a longtime sponsoring editor of *Economic Issues Today* at St. Martin's Press (before St. Martin's dropped its college economics line), for signing the book with its new publisher, M.E. Sharpe, Inc. And, as with each new edition, the senior author feels duty-bound to note the kind and thoughtful encouragement of Bertrand Lummus, then the college editor at St. Martin's, that made it possible for EIT to see the light of day in the first place. Similarly, the senior author wishes to acknowledge the efforts of Paula Franklin and Emily Berleth, whose extraordinary editorial skills in the early editions of the work have survived, both directly and indirectly, right down to the current version. All of the authors are indebted to Peter Coveney, the executive editor of M.E. Sharpe, for shepherding us through the preparation and publication of the sixth edition. We also acknowledge the inspired efforts of Sean Culhane, economics editor, who joined the project in midstream with admirable vigor and interest in its success.

_____ **Part 1**

Introduction

Alternative Economic Philosophies

A Survey of Conservative, Liberal, and Radical Critiques

The ideas of economists, both when they are right and when they are wrong, are more powerful than is commonly understood. Indeed, the world is ruled by little else. Practical men, who believe themselves to be quite exempt from any intellectual influences, are usually the slaves of some defunct economist. Madmen in authority, who hear voices in the air, are distilling their frenzy from some academic scribbler of a few years back.

John Maynard Keynes, 1936

A Beginning Note to the Student

At the time of this writing, the American economy is humming along just a few months shy of attaining a new record: the longest continuous expansion in the nation's history. By virtually any known standard of economic measurement, the national economy is doing very, very well. Unemployment is at a twenty-five-year low. Prices are stable. Economic growth, though not at a record-setting pace, is respectable. And the stock market continues to push upward, regularly setting new record highs.

Given such prevailing economic conditions, the authors, when they occasionally forget the capriciousness of history, sometimes ponder whether this book's title will be entirely understood by its readers. Indeed, some readers uninitiated into the mysteries of the discipline of economics may find the title perplexing. After all, what "economic issues" actually exist today? But, alas, such questioners will quickly learn that, even in the best of times, economists are quite adept at putting together long agendas of ongoing economic problems. These are often matters that have not yet been addressed even if we are in the middle of a long prosperity, while some of them are problems that will certainly emerge after prosperity fades a bit, as it always does.

A discerning would-be initiate to economics may also wonder about the subtitle to *Microeconomic Issues Today*. Even if there are unresolved economic issues, how is it possible that economists are of differing opinions as to how to address these problems? How can a respected field of social scientific inquiry be divided by matters of outlook that produce "alternative approaches" to the agenda of economic issues? These latter questions on differing approaches to economic reasoning, unlike the earlier one on economic issues themselves, are not easily or quickly answered. And, as the reader will learn, these are the *real questions* this book attempts to explain.

When Economists Disagree

Early in 1997, George Soros, financial capitalist extraordinaire, raised a mild firestorm among professional American economists and American political and economic commentators by publishing a piece in the *Atlantic Monthly* magazine. Soros was a multibillionaire who had made his fortune specializing in international currency speculation. By all outward appearances, he was the quintessential model of the success that free-market economic conditions can accord its more diligent practitioners. Yet, in his essay, Soros chose to question whether the rock-bottom assumptions of market theory were properly founded. In so doing, he was attacking the prevailing opinion of the economics profession and its many supporters, namely the view that conventional economic theory is a reasonably "scientific" explanation of how an ideal economy ought to operate.

George Soros was not yet to the point of attacking all aspects of market economics. However, in defending his larger view on the limits of free-market theory, he observed, "Markets are the best machines for correcting individual errors, but government intervention and collective action are needed to protect common interests and correct inequities in the capitalist system."

In the wake of the Soviet Union's collapse in 1992, at a time when market theory was enjoying growing support everywhere in the world, and precisely as a Democratic American president was agreeing with his Republican foes that "the era of big government" was over, Soros's statements briefly made big waves. The shock was all the greater because Soros was also striking at the underlying belief system of conventional economic theory. As he put it, "Laissez-faire ideology—which holds that the common interest is best served when each individual pursues his particular interest—is inadequate for holding our open society together." Accordingly, Soros was not just disagreeing with mainstream economists on a matter of policy emphasis, he was questioning the philosophical foundations of mainstream thinking.

It was a provocative challenge, and a lot of "nonmainstream economists" found themselves in the awkward position of agreeing with the observations of a wealthy capitalist.

True, the Soros affair was one of those increasingly frequent "mini-news" events that bubble up suddenly and quickly recede from journalistic and public notice. Yet, the issues it raised are not likely to go away, regardless of the extent, or lack, of continued public interest in George Soros's particular economic views. The fact remains, despite the apparent singlemindedness of most economic thinkers, that real differences of opinion and ideological perspective persist on how an "ideal" economy should operate. The old economic debates of the 1960s, 1970s, and 1980s between Conservative, Liberal, and Radical advocates perhaps have subsided as matters of prominent public and professional concern, but they have not passed out of existence.

It is well for the reader to remember that throughout the long history of human efforts to understand and explain economic matters, disagreement rather than consensus has been the rule. In a nation that puts great stock in consensus building as the ultimate tool of governance and the principal device for sustaining social order, this may be a disconcerting fact. In any event, it is one we should understand. At this writing, at a time of considerable national economic prosperity, real differences of political and economic opinion still circulate. And, as we should know from the historical record, "economic prosperity" itself has always been a transitory condition; when it fades, debate over alternative economic policies often becomes heated.

When that debate takes place, squabbling among economists over policy alternatives can scarcely be hidden from the public, and such disagreement can be downright unsettling. It often comes as a rude surprise to the person on the street, who, although paying due professional respect to economists, still sees the economist as a kind of mechanic. When one's car does not start, the car owner expects (at least hopes) that the diagnosis of mechanical trouble given at one garage is exactly the same as what will be heard at any other. If there is one mechanical problem, there should be one mechanical solution. The moral of this comparison is that the study of economics is more than studying a repair manual, and economists are not mechanics.

The Role of Ideology

How is such disagreement possible? Isn't economics a science? Economists' answers to that question vary. A common and reasonable enough response is simply that scientists disagree too. While there is much truth to such an answer, it really begs the question. Plainly, the "dismal science" of economics is not a science like physics. Whereas economists may sometimes talk about the laws of supply and demand as if they were eternal verities like the law of gravity, there is abundant anthropological and historical evidence that many societies have behaved quite contrary to the laws of supply and demand.

To be sure, economists employ (or at least should employ) the rigor of scientific method and quantitative techniques in collecting data, testing hypotheses, and offering reasonable conclusions and predictions. However, economists deal with different "stuff" from that of their colleagues in the exact sciences. Their data involve human beings and their laboratory is a world of behavior and perception that varies with time and place. On top of this, economists, like all social scientists, are called on to answer a question not asked of those in the "pure" sciences: "What *ought* to be?" Astronomers, for instance, are not asked what *ought* to be the gravitational relationships of our universe. That would be a nonsense question. Economists, however, cannot evade making some determinations about optimal prices, optimal income distribution, and so forth. Their decisions, while perhaps based on a genuine effort at neutrality, detachment, and honest evaluation of the available evidence, finally must be a matter of interpretation, a value judgment based on their own particular world views. To put the point directly: *Economics, as a study of human behavior, cannot avoid value judgments. Struggle as it may, economics as a discipline is never free from ideology.*

The early economists of the eighteenth and nineteenth centuries—Adam Smith, David Ricardo, John Stuart Mill, and especially the heretic Karl Marx—perceived economics as merely part of a broader political-economy context, but this view had largely been abandoned by the end of the nineteenth century. By the middle of the twentieth century, the economics profession generally approached "ideology" as if it were a dirty word, unprofessional, or, at the very best, too troublesome to deal with. The emphasis was on theoretical tools, considered both universal and neutral. All this changed in the 1960s and 1970s when well-known American economists thrust themselves into the powerful debates then sweeping American society. Their views on the war in Vietnam, poverty, civil rights, the extent of government power, the environmental crisis, the oil embargo, the causes of "stagflation," high technology versus smokestack industries, and much more could be heard regularly on television talk shows and miniseries or read in the columns of weekly newsmagazines. Often there was the pretension that this "talking out of church" had little impact on the body of "professional" theory and judgment, but the pretension was unconvincing. For good or ill, the genie was out of the bottle, and the economics profession had again become involved in politics and in recommending political courses of action to pursue economic objectives.

Initially, through the 1960s and into the early 1970s, prevailing opinion among economic reasoners upheld a Liberal perspective on political economy, advocating an active interventionism by government to "correct and improve" the workings of the economy. However, during the late 1970s, this consensus began to break down as the national economy slipped into a long period of sagging growth, rising unemployment, and escalating inflation. In its place, a new consensus began to build on behalf of a Conservative, minimum-government approach to political and economic matters. As the Liberals' star fell and the Conservatives' rose, the intensity and bitterness of economic and political argument sharpened. Although the shrillness of the ideological debate calmed a bit during the Reagan years—no doubt a by-product of the long economic expansion that began in late 1982—the past four decades of shifting ideological perspectives have left their mark on the economics profession. To a considerable extent, the ordinary economics textbook illustrates this point. While economics texts continue to do what such books have always done, namely, to introduce the reader to a generally agreed-on body of theoretical and analytical techniques and tools that constitute the study of economics, most have also found it necessary to identify and discuss the alternatives of Liberals, Conservatives, and, sometimes, even Radicals in the practical extension of economic analysis to actual policy-making situations.

The significance of all this should not be lost on the beginning student of economics. Though many economists may stress the value-free nature of their studies, and of economics in general, common sense and observation suggest that this is at best a vastly exaggerated claim. The content and application of economic reasoning are determined ultimately by the force of what economists believe, not by an independent and neutral logic. But to say that economics is a matter of opinion is not to say that it is just a study of relatively different ideas: Here's this view and here's that one and each is of equal value. In fact, opinions are not of equal value. There are good opinions and there are bad ones. Different economic ideas have different consequences when adopted as policy. They have different effects—now and in the future. As we confront the various policy solutions proposed to deal with the many crises now gnawing deep into our economy and society, we must make choices. This one seems likely to produce desired outcomes. That one does not. No other situation is consistent with a free and reasoning society. Granted it is a painful situation, since choice always raises doubts and uncertainty and runs the risk of wrong judgment, but it cannot be evaded.

This book is intended to focus on a limited number of the hard choices that we must make. Its basic premise is that economic judgment is fundamentally a matter of learning to choose the best policy solution among all possible solutions. The book further assumes that failure to make this choice is to underestimate the richness and importance of the economic ideas we learn and to be blind to the fact that ideas and analysis do indeed apply to the real world of our own lives.

On Sorting Out Ideologies

Assuming that we have been at least partially convincing in our argument that economic analysis is permeated by ideological judgment, we now turn to examine the varieties of ideology common to American economic thought.

In general, we may characterize the ideological position of contemporary economics and economists as Conservative, Liberal, or Radical. These, the same handy categories that evening newscasters use to describe political positions, presumably have some meaning to people. The trouble with labels, though, is that they can mean a great deal and, at the same time, nothing at all. At a distance the various political colors of Conservative, Liberal, and Radical banners are vividly different. Close up, however, the distinctiveness blurs, and what seemed obvious differences are not so clear. For instance, there is probably *not* a strictly Liberal position on every economic issue, nor are all the economists who might be generally termed "Liberal" consistently in agreement. The same is true in the case of many Radical or Conservative positions as well. Unless we maintain a certain open-endedness in our categorizing of positions, the discussion of ideological differences will be overly simple and much too rigid. Therefore, the following generalizations and applications of ideological typologies will attempt to isolate and identify only "representative" positions. By doing this we can at least focus on the differences at the center rather than on the fuzziness at the fringes of these schools of thought.

We are still left with a problem. How do you specify an ideological position? Can you define a Radical or a Liberal or a Conservative position? The answer here is simple. As the British economist Joan Robinson once observed, an ideology is like an elephant—you can't define an elephant, but you should know one when you see it. Moreover, you should know the difference between an elephant and a horse or a cow without having to resort to definitions.

There is a general framework of thought within each of the three ideological schools by which we can recognize them. Thus we will not "define" the schools but merely describe the salient characteristics of each. In all the following, the reader is urged to remember that there are many varieties of elephants. Our specification of a particular ideological view on any issue is a representative model—a kind of average-looking elephant (or horse or cow). Therefore, the Conservative view offered on the problem of federal deficits, for instance, will probably not encompass all Conservative thought on this question. However, it should be sufficiently representative so that the basic Conservative paradigm, or world view, can be distinguished from the Radical or Liberal argument. Where truly important divisions within an ideological paradigm exist, the divisions will be appropriately noted and discussed.

The Conservative Paradigm

What is usually labeled the Conservative position in economic thought and policy making was not always "conservative." Conservative ideas may be traced to quite radical origins. The forebears of modern Conservative thought—among them England's Adam Smith (1723–1790)—were not interested in "conserving" the economic order they knew but in destroying it. In 1776, when Smith wrote his classic *Wealth of Nations,* England was organized under a more or less closed economic system of monopoly rights, trade restriction, and constant government interference with the marketplace and individuals' business and private affairs. This system, known as mercantilism, had been dominant in England and, with slight variations, elsewhere on the Continent for over 250 years.

Adam Smith's Legacy

Smith's remedy was simple enough: Remove all restrictions on commercial and industrial activity and allow the market to work freely. The philosophical basis of Smith's argument rested on his beliefs that (1) all men had the natural right to obtain and protect their property; (2) all men were by nature materialistic; and (3) all men were rational and would seek, by their own reason, to maximize their material well-being. These individualistic tendencies in men would be tempered by competition in the marketplace. There, men would have to compromise with one another to gain any individual satisfaction whatsoever. The overall effect of these compromises would ultimately lead to national as well as individual satisfaction. Competition and self-interest would keep prices down and production high and rising, as well as stimulate product improvement, invention, and steady economic progress. For this to happen, of course, there would have to be a minimum of interference with the free market—no big government, no powerful unions, and no conspiring in trade. Smith's position and that of his contemporaries and followers was known as "Classical Liberalism." The Conservative label now applied to these views seems to have been affixed much later, when Smith's heirs found themselves acting in the defense of a status quo rather than opposing an older order.

Thus modern capitalist economic thought must trace its origins to Adam Smith. While this body of thought has been built on and modified over the past 200 years, the hand of Adam Smith is evident in every conventional economics textbook. Common sense tells us, however, that a lot has changed since Smith's day. Today business is big. There are labor unions and big government to interfere with his balanced free market of equals. His optimistic view of a naturally growing and expanding system is now replaced by growth problems and by a frequent dose of pessimism in some glances toward the future. Nevertheless, modern Conservatives, among contemporary defenders of capitalism, still stand close to the ideals of Adam Smith.

Modern Conservative thought is anchored in two basic philosophic ideas that distinguish it from Liberal and Radical positions. First, the market system and the spirit of competition are central to proper social organization. Second, individual rights and freedoms must be unlimited and uninfringed.

Conservatives oppose any "unnatural" interference in the marketplace. In particular, the Conservative views the growth of big government in capitalist society as the greatest threat to economic progress. Milton Friedman, Nobel laureate and preeminent figure in the Conservative Chicago school, has argued that government has moved from being merely an instrumentality necessary to sustain the economic and social order to becoming an instrument of oppression. Friedman's prescription for what "ought to be" on the matter of government is clear:

> A government which maintained law and order, defined property rights, served as a means whereby we could modify property rights and other

rules of the economic game, adjudicated disputes about the interpretation of the rules, enforced contracts, promoted competition, provided a monetary framework, engaged in activities to counter technical monopolies and to overcome neighborhood effects widely regarded as sufficiently important to justify government intervention, and which supplemented private charity and the private family in protecting the irresponsible, whether madman or child—such a government would clearly have important functions to perform. The consistent liberal is not an anarchist.*

The antigovernmental position of Conservatives in fact goes further than merely pointing out the dangers to individual freedom. To Conservatives the growth of big government itself causes or worsens economic problems. For instance, the growth of elaborate government policies to improve the conditions of labor, such as minimum-wage laws and Social Security protection, are seen as actually harming labor in general. A wage higher than that determined by the market will provide greater income for some workers, but, the Conservative argument runs, it will reduce the total demand for labor, and thus dump many workers into unemployment. As this example indicates, the Conservative assault on big government is seen not simply as a moral or ethical question but also in terms of alleged economic effects.

Another unifying feature of the representative Conservative argument is its emphasis on individualism and individual freedom. To be sure, there are those in the Conservative tradition who pay only lip service to this view, but for true Conservatives it is the centerpiece of their logic. As Friedman has expressed it:

> We take freedom of the individual . . . as the ultimate goal in judging social arrangements. . . . In a society freedom has nothing to say about what an individual does with his freedom; it is not an all-embracing ethic. Indeed, a major aim of the liberal [here meaning Conservative as we use the term] is to leave the ethical problem for the individual to wrestle with.**

Modern Conservatives as a group exhibit a wide range of special

---

*Milton Friedman, *Capitalism and Freedom* (Chicago: University of Chicago Press, 1962), p. 34.
**Ibid., p. 12.

biases. Not all are as articulate or logically consistent as Friedman's Chicago school. Many are identified more readily by what they oppose than by what they seem to be for. Big government, in both its micro-economic interferences and its macroeconomic policy making, is the most obvious common enemy, but virtually any institutionalized inter-ference with individual choice is at least ceremonially opposed.

Some critics of the Conservative position are quick to point out that most modern-day Conservatives are not quite consistent on the question of individual freedom when they focus on big business. In fact, until comparatively recently, Conservatives usually did demand the end of business concentration. Like all concentrations of power, it was viewed as an infringement on individual rights. The Conservative Austrian economist Joseph Schumpeter argued that "Big Business is a half-way house on the road to Socialism." The American Conservative Henry C. Simons observed in the depressed 1930s that "the great enemy to de-mocracy is monopoly." Accounting for the change to a more accommo-dating position on big business is not easy. Conservatives offer two basic reasons. First, big business and the so-called monopoly problem have been watched for a long period of time, and the threat of their power subverting freedom is seen as vastly overstated. Second, by far the larger problem is the rise of big government, which is cited as the greatest cause of business inefficiency and monopoly abuse. Another factor that seems implied in Conservative writing is the fear of commu-nism and socialism. To direct an assault on the American business system, even if existing business concentration were a slight impedi-ment to freedom, would lay that system open to direct Radical attack. How serious this supposed contradiction in Conservative logic really is remains a matter of debate among its critics.

The Recent Resurgence of Conservative Economic Ideas

In the United States, until the drab years of the Great Depression, what we now call "Conservative economics" *was* economics, period. Except for an occasional voice challenging the dominant wisdom, usually to little effect, few economists, political leaders, or members of the public at large disagreed greatly with Adam Smith's emphasis on individual freedom and on a free market economic condition.

The Depression years, however, brought a strong reaction to this kind of political and economic thinking. Many—perhaps most—of the millions of Americans who were out of work in the 1930s and the millions more who hung on to their jobs by their teeth came to believe that a "free" economy was simply one in "free fall." While most staunch Conservatives complained bitterly about the abandonment of market economics and the "creeping socialism" of Franklin Roosevelt's New Deal, they had few listeners. For thirty-two of the next forty-eight years after FDR's election in 1932, the White House, and usually the Congress, was in "Liberal" Democratic hands. For Conservatives, however, perhaps the greater losses were in the universities, where the old free market "truths" of Adam Smith and his disciples quickly fell out of style. In their place, a generation of professors espoused the virtues of the "New Economics" of John Maynard Keynes and the view that a capitalist economy "requires" government intervention to keep it from destroying itself.

Driven to the margins of academic and political influence by the 1970s, the Conservatives seemed in danger of joining the dinosaur and the dodo bird as an extinct species. However, by the late 1970s, in the aftermath of Vietnam and the Watergate scandal and in a period when nothing government did seemed able to control domestic inflation and unemployment problems, there developed a growing popular reaction against government in general. As more and more Americans came to believe that government economic and social interventions were the cause of the nation's maladies, the Conservative ideology took off again under its own power.

In 1980, the Conservative economic and political paradigm succeeded in recapturing the White House. Ronald Reagan became the first president since Herbert Hoover to come to office after a private-sector career. There was no doubting Reagan's philosophical commitment to the principles of a free enterprise economy.

As might be expected, Conservatives found themselves facing a difficult situation. Implementing a free market policy was, of course, much easier to accomplish in theory than in the real world—especially in a world vastly more complex than that envisioned by Adam Smith. "Reaganomics," the popular catchword for the new brand of Conservative economics, was quickly and sorely tested as the economy slipped into a deep recession in late 1981. To both friendly and hostile critics, Conservatives responded that quick solutions were not possible since the economic debris of a half-century needed to be swept aside before the economy could be reconstructed. Despite the fact that Reaganomics proved to be somewhat less than an unqualified success (indeed, a good many Conservatives would now call it a failure), the Reagan years were a time of moderate but sustained economic boom—the longest peacetime boom in American history. Despite some dark clouds—the near-tripling of the federal debt, a worsening international trade situation, and a precipitous stock market collapse in 1987—the Reagan–Bush 1980s remained, in economic terms, a comparatively bright period in American economic history. Meanwhile, the collapse of communism in Eastern Europe and the Soviet Union and the Soviet bloc's shift toward a more open economic and political system in the last years of the decade could only be counted as frosting on Conservatives' ideological cake. As America approached the end of the century, Conservatives basked in the sunlight of success. Important for our study is the fact that a wide range of Conservative economic ideas and political perspectives that had been shunned in serious academic debates for over forty years have again made their way back into economics textbooks.

Indeed, the rise and refurbishing of market-based economic theory—and not simply in the United States—in the last decade or two of the twentieth century is one of the most important recent developments in economics. For today's young reader, who probably believes that market-based doctrine *is* economics, it may be difficult to believe that Conservative thinking in both economic theory and policy making was, not so many years ago, without much influence in the economics profession. That fact is a good one to keep in mind. It illustrates something that is often overlooked: the prevailing ideological mood, what we might call "the conventional wisdom," is ever subject to change and reevaluation.

The Liberal Paradigm

According to a national poll, Americans tend to associate the term *Liberal* with big government, Franklin Roosevelt, labor unions, and welfare. Time was, not too long ago, when Liberal stood not just as a proud appellation but seemed to characterize the natural drift of the whole country. At the height of his popularity and before the Vietnam War toppled his administration, Lyndon Johnson, speaking of the new Liberal consensus, observed:

> After years of ideological controversy, we have grown used to the new relationship between government, households, business, labor and agri-

culture. The tired slogans that made constructive discourse difficult have lost their meaning for most Americans. It has become abundantly clear that our society wants neither to turn backward the clock of history nor to discuss the present problems in a doctrinaire or partisan spirit.*

Although what we will identify as the Liberal position in American economic thought probably still is alive and well in the teaching and practice of economic reasoning (as we shall see, even some Conservatives have adopted elements of the Liberal analysis), the Liberal argument is undergoing considerable changes. These changes, however, are more cosmetic than basic, and the central contours of Liberal belief are still visible.

The "Interventionist" Faith

Whereas Conservatives and Radicals are comparatively easily identified by a representative position, Liberals are more difficult to identify. In terms of public policy positions, the Liberal spectrum ranges all the way from those favoring a very moderate level of government intervention to those advocating broad government planning of the economy.

Despite the great distance between the defining poles of Liberal thought, several basic points can be stated as unique to the Liberal paradigm. Like their Conservative counterparts, Liberals are defenders of the principle of private property and the business system. These, however, are not categorical rights, as we observed in the Conservative case. Individual claims to property or the ability to act freely in the marketplace are subject to the second Liberal principle—that social welfare and the maintenance of the entire economy supersede individual interest. In a vicious condemnation of what we would presently call the Conservative position, John Maynard Keynes directly assaulted the philosophy that set the individual over society. Keynes argued:

> It is not true that individuals possess a proscriptive "natural liberty" in their economic activities. There is no "compact" conferring perpetual rights on those who Have or on those who Acquire. The world is not so governed from above that private and social interest always coincide. It

---

*The Economic Report of the President, 1965 (Washington, DC: U.S. Government Printing Office, 1965), p. 39.

is not a correct deduction from the Principles of Economics that enlightened self-interest always operates in the public interest. Nor is it true
that self-interest generally is enlightened; more often individuals acting
separately to promote their own ends are too ignorant or too weak to
attain even these. Experience does not show that individuals, when they
make up a social unit, are always less clear-sighted than when they act
separately.*

To the Liberal, then, government intervention in, and occasional
direct regulation of, aspects of the national economy is neither a violation of principle nor an abridgement of "natural economic law." The
benefits to the whole society from intervention simply outweigh any
"natural right" claims. The forms of intervention may vary, but their
pragmatic purpose is obvious—to tinker and manipulate in order to
produce greater social benefits.

Government intervention in the economy dates from the very begin-
nings of the nation, but the Progressives of the early twentieth century
were the first to successfully urge an extensive and systematic elaboration of governmental economic powers. In response to the excesses of
giant enterprises in the era of the Robber Barons, the Progressives
followed a number of paths in the period from 1900 to 1920. One was
the regulation of monopoly power, to be accomplished either through
antitrust prosecutions to restore competition or through the use of independent regulatory commissions in cases where a "break them up"
policy was undesirable (for instance, railroads and other firms possess-
ing *public utility* characteristics). A second was *indirect* business regulation effected by such Progressive developments as legalization of
unions, the passage of social legislation at both the federal and state
levels, tax reforms, and controls over production (for example, laws
against food adulteration)—all of which circumvented the power of
business and subjected it to the public interest.

Although the legislation and leadership of the administrations of
Theodore Roosevelt, William Howard Taft, and Woodrow Wilson
went a long way in moderating the old laissez faire ideology of the
previous era, actual interference in business affairs remained slight
until the Great Depression. By 1933 perhaps as many as one out of

---

*John M. Keynes, "The End of Laissez Faire," in *Essays in Persuasion* (New
York: Norton, 1963), p. 68.

every three Americans was out of work (the official figures said 25 percent), business failures were common, and the specter of total financial and industrial collapse hung heavy over the whole country. In the bread lines and shanty towns known as "Hoovervilles" as well as on Main Street, there were serious mutterings that the American business system had failed. Business leaders, who had always enjoyed hero status in the history books and even among ordinary citizens, had become pariahs. Enter at this point Franklin Roosevelt, the New Deal, and the modern formulation of "Liberal" government–business policies. Despite violent attacks on him from the Conservative media, FDR pragmatically abandoned his own conservative roots and, in a bewildering series of legislative enactments and presidential decrees, laid the foundation of "public interest" criteria for government regulation of the marketplace. *Whatever might work was tried.* The National Recovery Administration (NRA) encouraged industry cartels and price setting. The Tennessee Valley Authority (TVA) was an attempt at publicly owned enterprise. At the Justice Department, Attorney General Thurman Arnold initiated more antitrust actions than all of his predecessors combined. And a mass of "alphabet agencies" was created to deal with this or that aspect of the Depression.

Intervention to protect labor and extensions of social welfare provisions were not enough to end the Depression. It was the massive spending for World War II that finally restored prosperity. With this prosperity came the steady influence of Keynes, who had argued in the 1930s that only through government fiscal and monetary efforts to keep up the demand for goods and services could prosperity be reached and maintained. Keynes's arguments for government policies to maintain high levels of investment and hence employment and consumer demand became Liberal dogma. To be a Liberal was to be a Keynesian, and vice versa.

Alvin Hansen, Keynes's first and one of his foremost proponents in the United States, could scarcely hide his glee in 1957 as he described the wedding of Liberal Keynesian policies with the older government interventionist position this way:

> Within the last few decades the role of the economist has profoundly changed. And why? The reason is that economics has become operational. It has become operational because we have at long last developed a mixed public–private economy. This society is committed to the

welfare state and full employment. This government is firmly in the driver's seat. In such a world, practical policy problems became grist for the mill of economic analysis. Keynes, more than any other economist of our time, has helped to rescue economics from the negative position to which it had fallen to become once again a science of the Wealth of Nations and the art of Political Economy.*

Despite the Liberal propensity for tinkering—either through selected market intervention or through macro policy action—most Liberals, like Conservatives, still rely on traditional supply-and-demand analysis to explain prices and market performance. Their differences with Conservatives on the functioning of the markets, determination of output, pricing, and so forth lie not so much in describing what is happening as in evaluating how to respond to what is happening. For instance, there is little theoretical difference between Conservatives and Liberals on how prices are determined under monopolistic conditions. However, to the Conservative, the market itself is the best regulator and preventive of monopoly abuse. To the Liberal, monopoly demands government intervention.

Varieties of Liberal Belief

As noted before, the Liberal dogma covers a wide spectrum of opinion. Moreover, the Liberal position has shifted somewhat in response to the 1970s' economic disappointments and certain successes of the Reagan years.

On the extreme "left wing" of the Liberal spectrum, economists such as Robert Heilbroner and John Kenneth Galbraith have long argued that capitalism as the self-regulating system analyzed in conventional economic theory simply does not exist. Heilbroner contends: "The persistent breakdowns of the capitalist economy, whatever their immediate precipitating factors, can all be traced to a single underlying cause. This is the anarchic or planless character of capitalist production."** For a time, this critical defect led Heilbroner to flirt with

---

*Alvin H. Hansen, *The American Economy* (New York: McGraw-Hill, 1957), p. 175.

**Robert Heilbroner, *The Limits of American Capitalism* (New York: Harper and Row, 1966), p. 88.

"central planning" as the only possible "cure." However, he has recently backed away from this position, holding instead that capitalism plus government regulation to provide periodic corrections has proved to be more durable than central planning efforts.

To the left-leaning and always iconoclastic John Kenneth Galbraith, who sees problems of technology rather than profit dominating the giant corporation, a more rational atmosphere for decision making must be created. In brief, the modern firm demands a high order of internal and external planning of output, prices, and capital. The interests of the firm and state become fused in this planning process, and the expanded role of Liberal government in the whole economy and society becomes obvious. While Galbraith has in the past maintained that he was a socialist, the Liberal outcome of his program is obvious in that he (1) never explicitly takes up the expropriation of private property, and (2) still accepts a precarious social balance between public and private interest.

Although Galbraith's Liberalism leads to an economy heavily reliant on planning, most Liberals stop well before this point. Having rejected the logic of self-regulating markets and accepted the realities of giant business enterprise, Liberals unashamedly admit to being pragmatic tinkerers—ever adjusting and interfering with business decision making in an effort to assert the changing "public interest." Yet all this must be done while still respecting basic property rights and due process. Under these arrangements, business regulation amounts to a protection of business itself as well as the equal protection of other interest groups in pluralist American society.

In the not-too-distant past, business itself adapted to and embraced this position. Whereas certain government actions might be opposed, the philosophy of government intervention in the economy was not necessarily seen as antibusiness. The frequent Conservative depiction of most Liberals as being opposed to the business system does not withstand the empirical test. For instance, in 1964 Henry Ford II organized a highly successful committee of business leaders for Liberal Lyndon Johnson, while Conservative Barry Goldwater, with Friedman as his adviser, gained little or no big-business support. However, the extent of government regulation soon reached a level that was wholly unacceptable to the private sector. In the late 1960s and early 1970s, a blizzard of environmental, job safety, consumer protection, and energy regulations blew out of Washington. Added to what was already on the ground, the new legislative snowfall seemed to many observers at the end of the 1970s about to bring American business to a standstill. Many who a decade before frankly feared the economic "freedom" of the Conservative vision now embraced that position.

The distress of economic "stagflation" in the 1970s (lower growth, rising unemployment, *and* price inflation), for which the Liberals seemed to have no programmatic cures, along with a growing popular sentiment against "big government" in general, drove Liberals from positions of political influence. Even within universities, the Liberal consensus began to collapse, with some former Liberal theorists deserting to the Conservative camp and most others adopting a lower profile in their teaching, writing, and research. Yet by the end of the 1980s, most of the analytical and policy positions associated with Liberal economic reasoning still survived—a bit subdued from the high-flying days of Kennedy's New Frontier and Johnson's Great Society but distinguishable nonetheless. Among the more reform-minded Liberal reasoners, the old economic agenda items—income distribution, discrimination, the environment, consumer protection, monopoly abuse, labor unions, structural shifts in the economy and their resulting dislocations—remained vital concerns in any policy-making effort. However, Liberal hopes for a fairly swift and sweeping resolution of these problems had diminished greatly from the expectations of the 1960s and early 1970s. The new realities of a slow-growth economy, massive federal deficits, reduced American competitiveness in world markets, and costly entitlement programs put serious constraints on even a visionary reformer's dedication to interventionism. But this commitment had not been extinguished. When the Eastern European Communist states toppled like dominoes and the long-time cold war confrontation with the Soviet Union seemed to move steadily toward a peaceful end, there was brave talk among Liberals of the prospects for a "peace dividend." The ending of the cold war was envisioned as freeing up vast sums for favored social agenda items that had long been shelved.

Meanwhile, in the business community, the old propensity to enlist government on the side of "improving" the stability of domestic markets was given new life in the face of rising foreign competition, the decline of certain basic industries, and the double frights provided by Black Monday (the sudden collapse of the stock market on October 19, 1987) and the savings-and-loan industry crisis. In particular, the last two events seemed to show that too much market freedom might not be as desirable as it sounded.

The present-day ambivalence of Liberals on the degree and type of intervention will be evident in our survey of economic issues in this book; nevertheless, this tendency should not be misunderstood. Specific Liberal approaches to problem solving may be debatable, but the essence of Liberal economics remains unchanged: *The capitalist economy simply requires pragmatic adjustment from time to time to maintain overall balance and to protect particular elements in the society.*

The Radical Paradigm

For most readers, specification of a Radical paradigm will seem to be a difficult and unfamiliar exercise. The "Right" and the "Left," or "Conservative" and "Liberal," identifications are used nightly on the television news and talk shows, and presumably these labels have self-evident political meaning to most viewers. The Radical label is not so well known, nor is it used very much by the media. For the most part, Americans are generally uninformed about the content and objectives of a Radical social outlook. Yet, in a variation on the old cliché about "familiarity breeding contempt," we find also that "ignorance breeds contempt," at least with regard to ideological matters. Quite simply, most Americans—even if they know little about a Radical ideological outlook—believe it to be essentially "wrongheaded" and, at bottom, "un-American." Nevertheless, there is a Radical tradition in American economic thought, and it needs to be understood.

The principal litmus test for accepting the Radical position requires the rejection of production-for-profit capitalism as an economic system—both the free-market capitalism of Conservatives and the regulated capitalism of Liberals. Such a minimum membership standard, needless to say, leads to the lumping of a large number of very different anticapitalist critiques into the Radical category. Nonetheless, there is an important shared outlook among true Radicals. The essence of this perspective is nicely illustrated by a comment made some years ago by Tony Benn, a political and ideological leader of the British Labour Party. Queried by an interviewer in 1992 as to what was going to happen to socialists around the world now that the Marxist–socialist regime in the Soviet Union had collapsed, Benn offered a pregnant response. "The real struggle," Benn observed, "was never between capitalism and socialism. It was and is between capitalism and democracy."

In Benn's remark lies the common core of contemporary Radical thought: *Radicals espouse a social and economic order in which institutions are expected to respond to people's needs and people are to be empowered politically and economically so as to ensure "democratic" outcomes.*

At such a general level of articulation, Radical ideology may appear deceptively benign. Who, after all, can be opposed to "empowering people"? However, the economic and political empowerment of people quickly takes on a more serious and, to some, more threatening meaning when the Radical analysis is examined in greater detail. As the Radical tradition understands the economic and social dynamic of societies, power is intricately connected to the ownership of property: Whoever owns or controls the use of a society's "things" invariably possesses political and economic power commensurate with such ownership or control. In capitalism, ownership of "things," particularly the things (capital) that produce other things, is disproportionately held in the hands of a comparative few. These owners of the means of production are seen by Radicals as exercising excessive influence for their own personal (or class) gain in the society's decisions about what will be produced, how that output will be produced, and who will share in this output. In our Radical paradigm, empowerment necessarily leads to limiting private and individual economic power and to increasing the social ownership and control of the things within a society. For most readers, a word should spring to mind: "socialism."

Socialism as a political, social, even religious outlook probably predates the rise of capitalism. And "socialism" is an umbrella that can cover a multitude of ideological tendencies. Utopian communitarians, Christian socialists, anarchists, Marxists, syndicalists, communists, guild socialists, and many other ideological variants can crowd under the socialist umbrella. The common thread to membership in any socialist tradition is acceptance of the advocacy for the social or community ownership of all, or most, of the means of production and for a societally determined standard for the distribution of the output of the society.

While it is pretty clear that all socialists would qualify as Radicals, it is by no means true that all Radicals see themselves as socialists. Partly, this is the case because "socialism" has long been and certainly remains a "dirty word" among most Americans—an ideological outlook that directly challenges the nation's historical proclivity to explain social and economic life in largely individualist terms. Partly, it reflects the fact that "socialism" is simply too big an umbrella, and therefore, includes a lot of ideological outlooks that, once you get past a few basic theoretical similarities, don't agree on important issues of specific programs and goals.

Moreover, many American Radicals are not political activists at all. For them, commitment to a Radical perspective is mostly an intellectual and analytical exercise aimed at attacking and revealing the deficiencies of conventional Conservative and Liberal thought. Their purpose is not to build an alternative political party, such as "socialism" has tended to become, but to supply an alternative critical analysis that Americans might act upon within the constraints of the existing political order. In any case, in specifying a Radical paradigm, it is wise to remember that membership includes many different marchers not necessarily listening to the same drummer, or at least not hearing the same beat even if there is a single drummer. But then again, the same can be said for Conservative and Liberal paradigms.

However, as a practical matter, an extended explanation of the Radical paradigm must be assigned an ideological starting point. And most, but surely not all, American Radicals would admit their intellectual debt to Karl Marx and his nineteenth-century critique of capitalism.

The Marxist Heritage

Since the Marxist critique is likely to be less familiar to many readers than the basic arguments of Conservatives or Liberals, it is necessary to be somewhat more detailed in specifying the Radical position. As will be quickly apparent, the Radical world view rests on greatly different assumptions about the economic and social order than those of the Conservatives and Liberals.

According to Marx's view, the value of a commodity reflects the real labor time necessary to produce it. However, under capitalism workers lack control of their labor, selling it as they must to capitalists. The workers receive only a fraction of the value they create—according to Marx, only an amount sufficient in the long run to permit subsistence. The rest of the value—what Marx calls "surplus value"—is retained by capitalists as the source of their profits and for the accumulation of capital that will increase both future production and future profit. As the appropriation of surplus value proceeds, with the steady transference of living labor into capital (what Marx called "dead labor"), capitalists face an emerging crisis. With more and more of their production costs reflecting their growing dependence on capital (machines) and with surplus labor value their only source of profit, capitalists are confronted with the reality of not being able to expand surplus appropriation. Unless they are able to increase their exploitation of labor—getting more output for the same, or less, wages paid—they face a falling rate of profit on their growing capital investment. Worse still, with workers' relatively falling wages and capitalists' relatively increasing capacity to produce, there is a growing tendency for the entire capitalist system to produce more goods than it can in fact sell.

These trends set certain systemic tendencies in motion. Out of the chaos of capitalist competitive struggles for profits in a limited market there develops a drive toward "concentration and centralization." In other words, the size of businesses grows and the number of enterprises shrinks. However, the problems of the falling rate of profit and chronic overproduction create violent fluctuations in the business cycle. Each depression points ever more clearly toward capitalist economic collapse. Meanwhile, among the increasingly impoverished workers, there is a steady growth of a "reserve army of unemployed"—workers who are now unemployable as production decreases. Simultaneously, increasing misery generates class consciousness and revolutionary activity among the working class. As the economic disintegration of capitalist institutions worsens, the subjective consciousness of workers grows to the point where they successfully overthrow the capitalist system. In the new society, the workers themselves take control of the production process, and accumulation for the interest of a narrow capitalist class ceases.

The Modern Restatement of Marx

Of necessity, the modern Radical's view of the world must lack the finality of Marx's predictions. Quite simply, the capitalist system has not self-destructed and, in fact, in a good many respects is stronger and more aggressive than it was in Marx's day. Although the present-day Radical may still agree with Marx's long-run predictions about the ultimate self-destructiveness of the capitalist order, the fact is that *relevant* Radicals must deal with the world as it is. While the broad categories of Marx's analysis are retained generally, Radical thought must focus on real-world, current conditions of capitalist society and present an analysis that goes beyond merely asserting the Marxist scenario for capitalist collapse. Useful economic analysis must be offered in examining contemporary problems.

The beginning point for modern Radical critiques, as it was also for Marx over a hundred years ago, is the unquenchable capitalist thirst for profits. This central organizing objective of all capitalist systems determines everything else within those systems. The Radical analysis begins with a simple proposition about how capitalists understand market activity:

> Total sales = total cost of materials and machinery used up in production + total wages and salaries paid + (- in the case of losses) total profits

Such a general view of sales, costs, and profits is, thus far, perfectly consistent with traditional accounting concepts acceptable to any Conservative or Liberal. However, the Radical's analytic mission becomes clearer when the proposition is reformulated:

> Total profits = total sales - total cost of materials and machinery used up in production - total wages and salaries paid

It now becomes evident that increasing profits depends on three general conditions: (1) that sales rise, *ceteris paribus* (all things being equal); (2) that production costs (composed of wage costs and material and machinery costs) decline, *ceteris paribus;* or (3) that sales increases at least exceed production cost increases. The capitalist, according to the Radical argument, is not simply interested in total profits but also in the "rate of profit," or the ratio of profits to the amount of capital the capitalist has invested.

With capitalist eyes focused on raising profits or raising profit rates, it becomes clear to Radicals which individual economic policies and strategies will be advanced by capitalists: *Every effort will be made to keep costs low,* such as reducing wage rates, speeding up the production line, introducing so-called labor-saving machines, seeking cheaper (often foreign) sources of labor and materials, and minimizing outlays for waste treatment and environmental maintenance. At the same time, *efforts will be made to keep prices high,* especially through the development of monopolistic price-making power on both a national and an international scale. In all these activities, capitalists will make every effort to use government economic intervention to their own advantage—both in domestic markets and in expanding capitalist hegemony into the world.

However, the effort of individual capitalists—either on their own or aided by government—to expand profit produces, taking the system as a whole, a crisis in obtaining profits. For instance, the capitalist goals of keeping wages low and prices high must lead to situations where workers as consumers simply cannot clear the market of available goods. Accordingly, the aggregate economy deteriorates into periodic recession or depression, with rising unemployment among workers and falling profits for capitalists. With capitalist support, a variety of government monetary and fiscal efforts may be employed to offset these ups and downs in the capitalist business cycle—in particular to improve the profit and profit-rate situations of capitalist enterprises. However, so-called mixed capitalism (a mixture of private-sector and government planning of the economy) cannot overcome the fundamental contradictions of a dominantly private, production-for-profit economy. And, of course, with the expansion of capitalism throughout most of the world, the capitalist crisis takes on international proportions. Quite as Marx predicted, the general economic crises deepen and occur more frequently. The search for profit becomes more frantic and more destructive to the lives of ever greater numbers of people living under capitalist hegemony throughout the world.

From the Radical point of view, periodic crisis in capitalism is not the result of excessive tinkering with the market system, as Conservatives claim; nor will the tendency toward crisis be contained by Liberal interventionism. *Periodic and deepening crisis* is *capitalism.*

Radical analysis is, of course, more penetrating than this short résumé can indicate. One further point that should be examined briefly is Marx's view of the relationship between a society's organization for production and its social relations. To Marx, capitalism was more than an economic system. Private values, religion, the family, the educational system, and political structures were all shaped by capitalist class domination and by the goal of production for private profit. It is important to recognize this tenet in any discussion of how Marxists—or Radicals with a Marxist orientation—approach contemporary social and economic problems. Marxists do not separate economics from politics or private belief. For instance, racism cannot be abstracted to the level of an ethical question. Its roots are seen in the capitalist production process. Nor is the state ever viewed as a neutrality able to act without class bias. Bourgeois democracy as we know it is seen simply as a mask for class domination.

Marx, in his early writings before his great work, *Capital,* had emphasized the "qualitative" exploitation of capitalism. Modern Radicals have revitalized this early Marx in their "quality of life" assaults on the present order. In these they emphasize the problems of worker alienation, commodity fetishism, and the wasteful and useless production of modern capitalism. The human or social problems of modern life are seen as rooted in the way the whole society is geared to produce more and more profits.

In addition to their Marxist heritage, modern Radicals derive much of their impulse from what they see as the apparent failure of Liberalism. Liberal promises to pursue policies of general social improvement are perceived as actions to protect only *some* interest groups. In general, those benefiting under Liberal arrangements are those who have always gained. The corporation is not controlled. It is more powerful than ever. Rule by elites has not ended, nor have the elites changed. Moreover, the national goals of the Liberal ethic—to improve our overall national well-being—stimulated the exploitation of poor nations, continued the cold war, and increased the militarization of the economy.

The Question of Relevance

Quite obviously, the Marxist prediction of capitalism's final collapse has not yet come to pass. In fact, Radicals—particularly those very closely associated with the Marxist tradition—are increasingly obliged to account for what many non-Radicals see as an historical turning away from all collectivist political economic alternatives with the rise of market economies in previously socialist states. These trends, along with certain internal analytical problems of Marxist analysis, are quite sufficient for most non-Radicals to consign the whole Radical paradigm to the garbage heap of worthless, worn-out ideas.

A thoughtful observer may question whether this is an entirely enlightened conclusion to reach. First, the tendency to lump Marxism and real-world Communist systems together as one and the same, while long a habit in the non-Communist as well as the Communist world, rests on a grossly inaccurate understanding of Marx's philosophy. Second, Marxism—at least as American Radical scholars have developed and used it—is more a way of looking at how our economy works than a prophecy of things to come. It is the technique of analysis rather than the century-old "truth" of Marx's specific analysis that counts.

A third point might also be worth considering. Freed of the Soviet millstone, Radical critiques, which were easily evaded during the Cold War epoch, might take on more meaning and appeal. Radicals no longer have to explain away the Soviet errors of authoritarian politics, decrepit bureaucracies, and failed planning before putting forth their own critique of contemporary capitalism and their own democratic–socialist programs. Moreover, and of increasing importance to the relevance of Radical arguments, the post-Soviet world economy has yet to show the robustness that the victors of the Cold War might have expected. Standing unchallenged in the world, capitalism and variants of capitalism may loom as larger targets for Radical attack than is generally appreciated. Consequently, it may be just a bit early to count out the Radical paradigm as non-Radicals are presently inclined to do.

As noted before, not all Radicals subscribe to all Marxist doctrine, but Marxism in one form or another remains the central element of the Radical challenge. Marx's fundamental contention that the system of private production must be changed remains the badge of membership in the Radical ranks. This sets Radicals apart from mainstream Conservative and Liberal economists.

Critics of Radicalism usually point out that Radical analyses are hopelessly negativistic. Radicals, they say, describe the problems of capitalism without offering a solution other than the end of the whole system. While there is much truth to this charge, we shall see in the following sections that indeed some solutions are offered. But even if their program is vague, Radicals would argue that their greatest contribution is in revealing the truth of the capitalist system.

Despite lessened political influence, modern Radical economic thought still looms as a logically important alternative to the more broadly supported Conservative and Liberal paradigms. The force of an idea is not dependent on the number of true believers. Were that the case, Conservative economic doctrine would have disappeared thirty years ago.

Applying the Analysis to the Issues

We have identified the three representative paradigms; now we will put them to use. The following selected Issues by no means exhaust the economic and political crises troubling the nation; nevertheless, they provide a good-sized sampling of the social agenda confronting us. The Issues presented here were selected because of their immediacy and representativeness in illustrating the diverse ideological approaches of Conservative, Liberal, and Radical economic analyses.

In each of the following Issues, the representative paradigms are presented in a *first-person advocacy approach.* The reader might do well to regard the arguments like those in a debate. As in a debate, one should be careful to distinguish between substantive differences and mere logical or debating strategies. Thus some points may be quite convincing whereas others seem shallow. However, the reader should remember that, shallow or profound, these are representative political economic arguments advanced by various economic schools.

The sequence in presenting the paradigms is consistent throughout the text: first Conservative, then Liberal, then Radical. In terms of the logical and historical development of contemporary economic ideologies, this sequence is most sensible; however, it is certainly not necessary to read the arguments in this order. Each one stands by itself. Nor is any ideological position intentionally set out as a straw man in any debate.

Readers should look at each position critically. They should test their own familiarity with economic concepts and their common sense against what they read in any representative case. Finally, of course, as students of economics and as citizens, they must make their own decisions. They determine who, if anyone, is the winner of the debate.

Because of space limitations, the representative arguments are brief, and some important ideas have been boiled down to a very few sentences. Also, within each of the three major positions there is a wide range of arguments, which may sometimes be at variance with one another. Conservatives, Liberals, and Radicals disagree among themselves on specific analyses and programs. For the sake of simplicity, we have chosen not to emphasize these differences but arbitrarily (although after much thought) have tried to select the most representative arguments. Each paradigm's discussion of an issue presents a critique of present public policy and, usually, a specific program proposal.

In all of the arguments, the factual and empirical evidence offered has been checked for accuracy. It is instructive in itself that, given the nature of economic "facts," they can be marshaled to "prove" a great variety of different ideological positions. Different or even similar evidence supports different truths, depending on the truth we wish to *prove.*

Problems in the Marketplace

Part 2 focuses on issues generally accepted by economists as *micro-economic* in their analysis. Microeconomics examines specific economic units—households, firms, industries, labor groups—and the behavior of these individual units.

The focal point of formal microeconomic analysis since its nineteenth-century origins has been the market. Accordingly, Part 2 looks at selected problems in the marketplace. Topics include problems of agricultural supply and demand, consumer market behavior, environmental economics, firm size, government regulation, income distribution, and government finance. Each topic presents some important dimension of market performance; each has been selected for its representative qualities in developing a broadened understanding of microeconomic problems within the contemporary American economy.

Responding to Market Outcomes

Competition or Protection for American Agriculture?

Farmers should raise less corn and more Hell.

Mary E. Lease, Kansas, 1890s

We produce too much food in this country.

Marty Strange, Farmer Advocacy Group, 1982

Because farmers are provided an incentive to make cropping decisions according to program rules rather than market signals, the [farm] programs reduce the responsiveness of U.S. agriculture to changes in world market conditions and reduce its international competitiveness.

Economic Report of the President, 1990

For eighteen years, the price of food has not kept up with the cost of farming.

Don Taus, South Dakota Farmer, 1998

The Problem

The teaching of economic reasoning usually begins with a general examination of the market model and, more particularly, with a consideration of how the market determines production, pricing, and resource allocation under conditions of pure competition. Such an introduction to economics presents the beginner almost immediately with a confusing irony. On the one hand, markets for agricultural goods would seem to be especially appropriate for illustrating the general conditions of competition because they are dominated by many small producers selling virtually identical products to a very broad range of consumers. Thus, agriculture should be a marvelously useful example of the market forces of supply and demand at work, and introductory textbooks invariably use wheat, corn, or some other farm product when they begin constructing simple analytical models.

In the real world, on the other hand, agricultural markets illustrate a quite contrary tendency. Here we do not find competition and free-flowing market forces, but rather some of the most elaborate efforts ever devised to insulate an industry from the market and to employ government intervention to promote private objectives. Agricultural output and pricing decisions actually are directly affected by a federal price-support program that has been in place in one form or another for sixty years. Meanwhile, a variety of government agencies provide emergency aid of staggering proportions. In fact, annual payments of emergency loans and other funds in excess of $30 billion or more per year were not uncommon a decade ago, as net farm income (in real dollars) hovered near the levels it had been in the Great Depression decade.

The condition of American agriculture has not always been one of unrelenting crisis, but the "farm problem" has been around, on and off again, for most of the twentieth century. The rhythm of farm fortune and misfortune has been like this: First, World War I created an exceptional demand for American farm products to feed soldiers and starving civilians. With rising prices resulting, farmers increased their output, but, in the 1920s and 1930s, after production increased, foreign demand for American

Figure 1.1. **Net Income of Farm Operators from Farming 1970–1996**

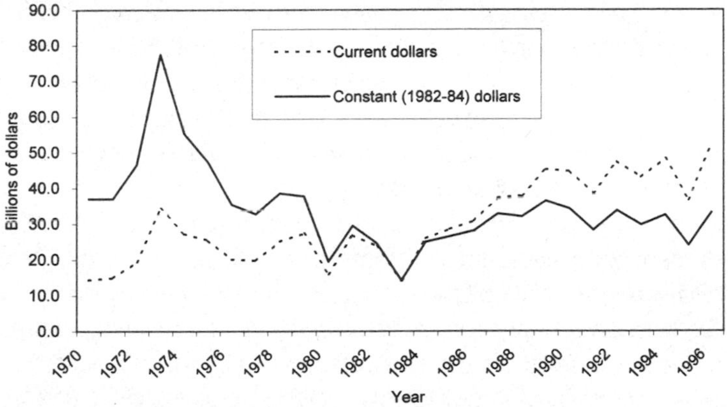

Source: Data from *Economic Report of the President, 1998.*

farm products declined and prices plummeted. The deepening depression after 1930 soon transformed the growing agricultural crisis into a full-blown catastrophe. With the coming of the New Deal in 1933, the federal government introduced numerous market interventions aimed at artificially raising or maintaining prices. These interventions included establishing a price-support system in which government guaranteed paying farmers the difference between the market price and an established "parity" (fair) price for their crops, as well as efforts to hold up the price of farm goods by paying farmers for taking some of their land out of production. These actions laid the economic and political foundations for what was to become a long-term, if not actually permanent, government intervention in agricultural markets. World War II pumped up demand and farm prices, but peace again brought tumbling prices and reliance on government support programs. Several Russian grain deals in the 1970s returned good times for a few years; however, farmers were soon caught up in new problems—a few of which were of their own making. Figure 1.1 illustrates the roller coaster ride that American farm income has taken since 1970.

As farm exports rose in the mid-1970s and farm prices and income followed, American farmers developed a false sense of newfound security. Planting "fencepost to fencepost" became common. Many farmers undertook considerable acquisitions of additional land and new equipment, swelling their mortgage and loan obligations. Farm debt tripled between 1973 and 1983. At first, few farmers paid much attention to the fact that interest rates on their new loans were high and rising during most of this period. The farm mood was upbeat, and many farmers thought they had finally escaped from the traditional boom-bust cycle of the agricultural economy.

But through the 1970s until bottom was hit in the 1980s, American farmers experienced a lot of "bust" and very little "boom." First, inflation got in its licks, as the general price expansion of the late 1970s pushed up fuel, machinery, and borrowing costs. Unable to pass these costs on in the form of higher prices, because overseas agricultural production was increasing and the prices of foreign food products were falling, American farmers saw their profit margins and net incomes squeezed. Through the 1970s and into the 1980s, American farmers' overseas sales declined, and cheaper foreign agricultural goods began to penetrate domestic markets.

However, by the mid-1990s, even in the face of several years of bad weather that adversely affected American agriculture, the hard times seemed to be lifting. When a new, Republican-dominated Congress took its seat in 1994, it promised to "get government out of farming." Briefly, it looked like the old government strategies of levying tariffs on imported goods, operating marketing boards, paying subsidies, setting output quotas, making payments for letting land lie idle, and much else that had become American farm policy suddenly would be washed away by congressional opponents of agricultural protection. But, in the Freedom to Farm Act of 1996, the final phasing out of agricultural support and subsidy programs was not to take place until 2002. And, scarcely two years after the act's passage, opposition was building among farmers and farm groups to the entire philosophy of the "Freedom to Farm" legislation.

The debate over agricultural policy remains an important issue and a profoundly significant theoretical question, since it goes to the very foundation of American economic belief; namely, do free and competitive markets work, or do they need constant repair and support by means of government intervention? Exactly how divided economists are on this question becomes apparent when we look at the policy alternative pro-posed by our three paradigms.

Synopsis

The Conservative position holds that the free operation of supply and demand is the correct and most effective determinant of agricultural prices. Liberals most frequently argue that an agricultural market left to itself is subject to wild cyclical fluctuation; thus a variety of government interventions are necessary to maintain reasonable order. Radicals see the American farm problem as a case of government being manipulated by agribusiness, with the result that government intervention has harmed both small farmers and ordinary consumers.

Anticipating the Arguments

- Why do Conservatives believe that most government efforts to help farmers by "artificially" raising crop prices actually hurt both farmers and consumers?
- What is the historical and economic foundation to the Liberal argument that farmers can't "depend" on unregulated farm markets?
- Why do Radicals believe that most farmers have been losers under both regulated and unregulated agricultural production in the United States?

THE CONSERVATIVE ARGUMENT

Discussions of the "American farm problem" almost always begin with a mistaken identification of what the problem really is. Most agricultural observers, including many economists writing on farm issues, suggest that there is something inherently unstable about American agriculture. Somehow, agriculture is presented as "proof" that the market economy simply does not work, that the free market forces of supply and demand break down. Conservatives agree that there is indeed a farm problem; however, that problem begins and remains in Washington, D.C., not in the corn and wheat fields of the Midwest or the commodities markets in Chicago. In other words, the American farm problem is not the result of some basic failure of the market, but rather the failure of federal policy to allow the market forces to work.

Policy Failure in Times of Surplus

Although many politicians and some economists may believe and act to the contrary, supply and demand remain the only effective determinants of prices and resource allocation. Of course, it is possible to contrive "desired" prices and output through a manipulated agricultural policy, but regardless of short-run success, such policies must produce serious misallocations and costs in the long run.

For a considerable period of time, at least since World War I, most economists have seen the American farm problem as a matter of rising productivity with comparatively stable or modestly increasing demand. The result in the marketplace was a general and persistent downward pressure on farm prices. The economic options under such conditions were either to let prices fall to whatever level they might reach or to maintain prices artificially. Due largely to political pressure from the farm lobby in the depressed 1930s, the government devised a potpourri of farm programs to keep prices up and supposedly guarantee a living income to the American farmer. Tariffs were slapped on foreign farm products. Certain "basic" farm products were guaranteed a government-paid "parity" price well above the going market price. Bureaucrats worked out production controls and acreage allotments, with the curious economic aim of paying producers not to produce.

These tinkerings with the market forces of demand and supply, however, did not produce order in agricultural markets. Each intervention, regardless of its noble intentions, increased agricultural dependence on government price-setting efforts and, at the same time, heightened market instability. For their own part, farmers paid less and less attention to production signals from the marketplace and relied increasingly on the government to bail them out whenever farm income showed signs of falling. With the government establishing minimum price levels (using either parity price or target price mechanisms) and standing ready either to buy surplus production (before the 1970s) or, more recently, to provide loans secured by surplus output, there has been little incentive to pay attention to market forces. Except for two brief interludes—during World War II, when America virtually fed the world, and after the early Russian grain deals in the 1970s—farm prices and the income of most farmers have been held up only by government manipulation of crop prices.

The Price of Failure

The Cost to Consumers

The benefits accruing to the farm lobby from government intervention have only recently become recognized as costs to the general public. Americans have paid for government subsidies, tariffs, and production controls in two ways: First, the price of food in general has been higher than it would otherwise have been in a "free" agricultural market. For most Americans over most of the past sixty years, this higher price presented few problems. With the steady rise in American standards of living, the artificially higher food prices seemed quite tolerable, and as food expenditures declined as a share of total consumer purchases during the post–World War II years, the farm lobby met little resistance in its efforts to expand market intervention. Not until the inflationary 1970s did Americans show signs of balking at rising farm prices, and even then most of their anger was aimed at grocery chains and other middlemen.

Second, Americans, in a sense, must pay for their food *twice*. Consumers are also taxpayers, and as such they are obliged to shoulder the cost of expensive government subsidies—direct payments and low-cost loans—to farmers. Moreover, they have had to pay for the maintenance of an elaborate bureaucracy developed to administer the various farm programs. As with the higher farm product prices, this hidden second price was for a very long time ignored by most taxpayers, a cost somehow obscurely buried in the federal budget. However, with pressure growing recently to reduce government spending and to reverse the growth of government debt, this previously concealed second charge for food became more obvious. By 1995, federal price support and other income programs for farmers were costing the average American family $300 per year—for an agricultural program aimed in the first place at keeping tabletop food prices artificially high.

Inability to Sell Overseas

Meanwhile, higher American farm prices closed off U.S. food products from world markets. Due to climate, soil, technology, and agricultural science, American agriculture has had an enormous advantage over the rest of the world in food production. This advantage, and the export income it would have created, was frittered away by programs aimed at keeping domestic prices relatively high. Precisely at a time when the United States faced a worsening balance of international payments (after World War II), the government pursued an agricultural program that denied the nation earnings it could have been making by exporting food.

The Russian grain deals of the mid-1970s brought a dramatic but brief reversal in agricultural export habits. In 1972, the Russians negotiated the purchase of 19 million metric tones of grain. For a number of years, Soviet leadership had been yielding to consumer pressure to produce more meat protein. Of necessity, this meant providing greater amounts of grain for beef in feeding lots. When the 1971 and 1972 crops failed to reach expectations, the Soviet leaders decided not to slaughter their beef herds or tell their people to eat potatoes and beets. They chose instead to buy U.S. grain and to allow their "protein program" to continue.

To growers and sellers, the "discovery" of the Russian market was a critical new direction for American agriculture, putting an end to the long era of chronic excess production, depressed prices, and dependence on government subsidy programs. By selling the equivalent of one-quarter of the 1972 crop, the Russian grain deal literally emptied American storage bins and grain elevators. This additional demand drove the prices of wheat from $1.70 per bushel in mid-1972 to $5.00 in 1973.

The trouble was, however, that commitment to free agricultural markets was unfamiliar, and when net farm income began to tumble in 1977 as the combined result of increases in production (a natural reaction to the increase in worldwide sales), a deepening worldwide recession, and worsening domestic inflation, farmers returned to their old habits. When the Agricultural Act was renewed in 1977, the farm lobby succeeded in setting target prices (the prices government would guarantee farmers through subsidies regardless of the going market prices) at about 25 percent higher than the existing world prices for most key crops. The "free market" experiment was over.

Insofar as government agricultural policy continues to "aid" farmers by artificially raising farm prices, farmers will be unable to exploit their efficiency and natural advantages in world food markets. Indeed,

Figure 1.2. **Changes in Farming, 1950–1996**

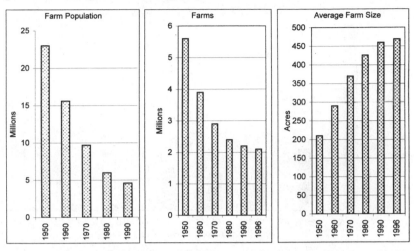

Source: Statistical Abstract of the United States, 1997 and data from the Bureau of the Census.

American farm prices are high enough to invite threats of agricultural imports.

Maintaining Production Inefficiencies

Before taking up the question of production inefficiencies resulting from interventionist farm policies, we need first to square with reality the myth of the lonely and hardworking individual agriculturist. The myth of the independent family farm is deeply ingrained in American popular belief and Liberal political posturing, and is the foundation of American farm policy. The irony is, however, that the small family farm has ceased to be an important supplier of foodstuffs. Figure 1.2 tells the story very quickly.

The farm population has fallen to about one-fifth of its 1950 level, while the number of farms has declined by more than half and average farm size has more than doubled over the same period. Figure 1.3 makes the point quite clearly: At present, 73 percent of the value of farm production is produced by just 17 percent of all operating farms. Moreover, less than 1 percent of all operating farms produce one-third of our food production.

The myth of the independent farmer is the basis for government

Figure 1.3. **Shares of Total Farm Sales by Farm Size, 1992**

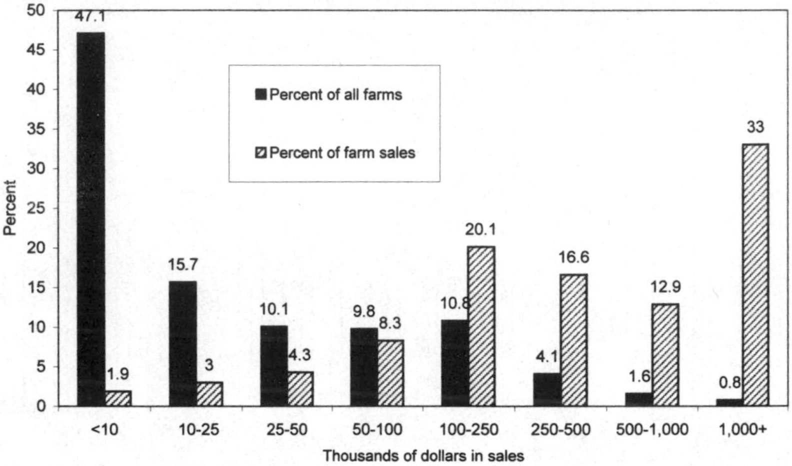

■ Percent of all farms

▨ Percent of farm sales

Source: U.S. Bureau of the Census, *1992 Census of Agriculture,* vol. 1.

subsidies—an effort to provide an income floor for the very poorest of farmers. The effect is to subsidize the least efficient farm producers at the very bottom of the agricultural ladder (two-thirds of government payments go to small farms that produce only a quarter of the nation's output) and very large farms that do not need it. This expensive agricultural welfare system has discouraged the out-movement of marginal agricultural producers who might better shift their resources to other productive pursuits. Worse still, subsidies paid to large and efficient farm producers act as restraints on improving their existing efficiency and productivity.

So long as we approach the farmer as if we were protecting a rare bird from extinction, we will not benefit from the practical forces of the marketplace. We will sustain at great economic cost farmers who should stop farming and, at the same time, hold back the application of business management methods and technological advances among the farm enterprises most capable of exploiting new techniques. We must recognize that farming is a business and, mythology notwithstanding, should be open to the forces of a production-for-profit economy, just like the manufacture of automobiles or personal computers.*

---

*Indeed, we should recognize the growing importance of business corporations in American agriculture. By the 1990s, 50,000 corporate farms, amounting to about 1 percent of all farms, produced more than a fifth of farm output in the United States.

Toward a New Policy Direction

A Conservative program for dealing with the nation's chronic agricultural problem is easily stated: *Let markets work.* This means ending all subsidies, special loan arrangements, crop control programs, target pricing, and other arrangements aimed at setting selling prices above free market prices.

Under the Freedom to Farm Act (1996), we are now on our way to restoring sanity to American agriculture. The phasing out of government pricing efforts by the year 2002 will drastically reduce agricultural prices and bring to an end an old and costly protectionist approach to American farming.

Falling agricultural prices (or at least a halt to their artificial rise) will have a number of salutary effects: First, it will be a direct benefit to American consumers. Second, it will expand American markets overseas. Lost revenues from lowered prices will be more than offset by expanded total sales. Third, the resulting emphasis on efficient and innovative use of productive resources in agriculture will create a strong, self-sufficient, and highly productive agricultural sector where the market actually directs resource inputs.

To be sure, reliance on the market will not be without some adjustment problems. Critics will be quick to point out the effect of short-term cycles in agriculture on production and prices: This year's high price causes next year's production to rise, increasing next year's supply faster than demand increases. The resultant lower prices lead to a reduction of supply in the next year and to a rise in prices, which in turn stimulate an increase in supply. According to many critics, this price instability perpetuates adversely effects alternately visited on consumers and then on farmers. The trouble with the argument is that no one has ever shown market-priced agricultural products to be more unstable than most other goods priced according to market forces of supply and demand. In fact, demand for agricultural goods is much more stable over time than demand for steel, automobiles, or even PCs. Moreover, a good deal of the volatility on the supply side is actually the result of government tinkering. There is a high probability that farm prices will fluctuate under a free market mechanism, but it is wrong to conclude that such fluctuations are undesirable. They are simply the market at work.

Certainly price fluctuations will pose problems for farmers long accustomed to prices rigged by the government. The less efficient

Table 1.1

U.S. Agricultural Productivity, 1800–1950

Crop	1800	1880	1920	1950
Wheat				
yield/acre (bu)	15	13	14	17
labor hours/100 bu	373	152	87	28
Corn				
yield/acre (bu)	25	26	28	39
labor hours/100 bu	344	180	113	39
Cotton				
yield/acre (bu)	147	179	160	283
labor hours/bale	601	318	269	126

Source: U.S. Bureau of the Census, *Historical Statistics of the United States,* Series K 83–97 (Washington, DC, 1960).

will find survival difficult. On the other hand, efficient family farms and farm corporations, applying the best production methods and determining output decisions on rational calculations of past *and* present market trends, should adjust quite nicely. Many small farm enterprises will fail, but this should be counted as no greater social loss than the disappearance of the corner butcher shop when supermarkets revolutionized food retailing. Nostalgia may have its virtues, but it can rarely be trusted for efficient allocation of resources and optimal pricing of outputs.

THE LIBERAL ARGUMENT

Conservatives are quite right in stating that the American farm problem has been largely one of gains in production consistently outstripping increases in demand. Throughout most of this century, food demand was essentially a function of domestic population increase. Until recently the United States has exported large quantities of food abroad only in time of war. Meanwhile, steady advances in agricultural technology and science have produced greater output and reduced human labor needs. Table 1.1. puts these gains in perspective.

Rising Production and Growing Crisis

Each unit of land has been producing greater yields as a result of new fertilizers and hybrid strains. At the same time, the application of greater capital has reduced substantially the number of worker-hours needed in production. By the 1930s, American farmers were the most productive in the world—and were going broke the fastest. It is easy enough for the Conservative devotee of the laws of supply and demand to say, "Leave things alone and let the devil take the hindmost." The fact is, excess agricultural production and falling prices affected people—a great number of people.

In 1930, about 44 percent of the U.S. population was classified as rural. About 57 million people still lived on farms or in small towns dependent on agriculture. At least 31 million were full-time farmers. To have adopted the Conservative proposal of letting these human resources "drop out" of farming if it didn't pay and find alternative employment would have been inhumane and stupid. In the Great Depression decade, there was no alternative employment. The exodus from farming (which did reduce the farm population to less than 10 million by 1972) would have been faster and would have created even greater employment problems for the general economy.

With this in mind, the New Deal policies of reducing farm migration through price supports, direct payments, and other subsidies (easy credit, electrification, and so on) were created. To be sure, these programs *did* artificially hold up farm prices and, in terms of subsidy costs, *did* pass the cost of the farm program on to taxpayers at large. But they also brought a degree of order to the agricultural sector and improved the income distribution inequities between farmers and nonfarmers. For example, 1934 farm income was only about one-third that of nonfarm income ($163 per year per person compared to $469 per year per person, respectively). By 1964, after nearly thirty years of New Deal–type "tinkering," annual farm income per person stood at $1,405 and nonfarm income at $2,318. Moreover, the supposed costs of federal farm subsidy programs have been vastly overstated. For instance, subsidies and support payments paid to farmers annually amount to less than 10 percent of all federally paid subsidies to the private sector.

It must be conceded that past American agricultural policy has had its failures. For instance, the improved income level of the farm sector, a noteworthy achievement, masks some other problems. The farm programs of the 1930s, 1940s, and 1950s could not halt the eventual decline of the family farm or the regional small farm in the Northeast. With greater application of technology and changes in farm production, farm employment (mostly family workers) fell from 7 million in 1970 to under 3 million in 1995. Although average farm income did improve relative to nonfarm income during the 1960s and 1970s, maldistribution of earnings within the farm sector increased. Large farms (those with annual sales of $100,000 or more) increased their share of agricultural markets from 17 percent in 1960 to more than 80 percent in 1995.

We easily can conclude, then, that the few big farms have been getting bigger, but that most remaining farmers still earn very modest incomes. In such a situation, it is quite likely that past farm subsidy programs and payments for nonproduction have provided the greatest gains for the large farm producer. However, even with these shortcomings, the earlier farm policies are defensible. They did raise and maintain average farm earnings above what a purely laissez-faire solution would have produced, thus strengthening agriculture in general. They mitigated the impact of the Depression on many farmers, and when farm out-migration did occur after World War II, the displaced farmers were more easily absorbed into a growing economy. The Conservatives' laissez-faire policy would have emptied rural America sooner, encouraged the growth of only the largest farms, and led to unacceptable human costs.

While past Liberal farm policies are historically defensible, it is apparent that America has moved into a new agricultural era demanding policy changes. The capital-intensive nature of agriculture is everywhere apparent, and the day of the small family farm is past. At the same time, the long-run future growth in world food demand is undeniable. These trends, however, are misunderstood by the free market advocates.

The Recent Failure of Market-Based Programs

Between 1972 and 1975, agricultural prices generally rose and price supports and any effort to restrict output were unnecessary and ill-advised. However, as the Agriculture and Consumer Protection Act of 1973 anticipated, high prices paid to farmers in the 1970s would not hold permanently. The 1973 act introduced the concept of target pricing. Under this arrangement, government announces a target price on a specified list of commodities. If the market price is below the target price, the government pays farmers the difference between what they would receive for selling their goods in the market and the targeted figure. According to such a plan, consumers would still enjoy the benefits of the lower market price, but farmers would be guaranteed a reasonable return on their crops. To prevent the very large producers from tapping the public treasury for outrageous subsidy payments, the 1973 law specified that no farmer should receive more than $20,000 in payment for any crop.

Although subsequent agricultural acts (the Agricultural and Consumer Protection Act is renewed every four years) have raised this per-farmer ceiling, the ceiling never was a very significant restriction because the larger farmers learned early on to "divide" their holdings among their relatives with each smaller "farm" qualifying for the maximum payments. Meanwhile, very small farmers were virtually unaffected by the restriction on payments and they continued to fail in large numbers. However, the target pricing and payment program did provide an important cushion for the middle-sized farms that are still the backbone of American agriculture.

If such payment programs, along with various loan programs, had not been in place in the middle and late 1980s, the disaster that struck American farming regions would have been much greater. More "free market" would have meant more farm agony. The early 1970s' experiment with reliance on supply and demand had introduced "fencepost-to-fencepost" planting and encouraged farmers to expand debt and mortgage obligations to heighten production. Meanwhile, the collapse of demand for American farm products could only be partly blamed on high agricultural prices and the strong U.S. dollar. Quite simply, even in a hungry world, effective demand for food did not keep pace with the growth in world food supply. It should be remembered that the high interest rates and rising costs confronting farmers in the early 1980s were not the farmers' fault nor the fault of farm policy. They were the outcome of a number of "supply shocks" (e.g., rising oil prices) that generated inflationary pressures. It was the Reagan administration's decision to fight this inflation with a "tight money" policy that drove up interest rates and forced massive bankruptcies in American agriculture. Without standby government payments and credit and loan programs, many more than the estimated one-third of American farmers would have been facing bankruptcy in the late 1980s.

What the Market Can't Do

Curiously, the cyclical swing of agricultural fortunes through the 1970s and 1980s was forgotten by policy-makers by the 1990s. With the passage of the Freedom to Farm Act of 1996, the nation adopted a farm policy that would eliminate price supports, target pricing, and virtually all other safety nets that had evolved to protect agriculture from the violent short-run fluctuations that forever attend agricultural markets.

The Conservative focus on long-run trends in agricultural markets is misleading, and their argument for "free" agricultural markets is simple-minded. A long-run trend is nothing more than the average of a cycle of short-run highs and lows. If short-run fluctuations are extreme, especially the lows, the agricultural sector will be torn apart. Resources forced out of agriculture in bad periods will not return quickly when prices later rise. A farm is not an enterprise that can be worked for a few years and then briefly retired until a boom "naturally" reappears. The land "blows away" if it isn't cultivated, and the equipment rusts and becomes obsolete. Neither the farmer nor the consumer, who would face violently fluctuating prices, should be subjected to the severity of short-run market readjustments. The laws of supply and demand, in fact, can be regulated to improve market outcomes.

Price support programs provide stability at a minimum cost. This, however, is not all that is required. Establishment of a crop reserve program for certain storable crops in good years as a hedge against drastic price increases in bad times or times of excessive demand would lead to price stabilization and more rational production planning. Various credit and loan programs must be available to finance planting and the purchase of farm equipment.

The object of such a farm policy should not be to sustain the mythical small farmer. Indeed, Conservatives are quite correct in pointing out the futility of such an objective. However, the Conservative argument on behalf of total reliance on market forces masks its real effect: The eventual domination of American agriculture by giant farm combines and corporations. The Liberal does not oppose that outcome because of some nostalgic attachment to a vanished past; rather, the Liberal opposes it because it could lead to the domination of American agriculture by a comparative handful of giant farm producers who can effectively raise prices by jointly controlling output. In the name of the free market, a monopolistically determined price system might indeed replace the mild interventions of government—to the considerable anguish of American consumers.

THE RADICAL ARGUMENT

When conventional economics textbooks reach for an example in discussions of "how supply and demand sets prices" or "how competition works," agricultural markets are usually cited. In the idealized models, at least, there are many small producers and consumers of homogeneous products who haggle and bargain until a fair and equitable price is established. For anyone vaguely familiar with the real-world conditions of American agriculture, the irony is heavy; nothing could be further from the truth. Perhaps because we start with such subtle deceptions when we talk about agricultural markets, we continue to deceive ourselves when we look for solutions to real farm problems. American agricultural affairs are dominated by a comparatively small number of giant producers, not by many small equal-sized farms, and prices are more the result of market power or government intervention than of the free market at work. Agriculture, as much as any sector of the economy, reveals the conflict between the professed ideal of a modified, production-for-profit system and the reality that a few benefit at the losses of many. The losers, of course, are small farmers and consumers in general.

The Old Policy: Help the Big Guys

While most farm programs between 1920 and 1973 were supposedly aimed at protecting the family farm and supporting the agricultural sector in general, they failed utterly to halt the concentration of agriculture into fewer and fewer hands. Programs of price supports and payments for nonproduction stimulated this concentration, since small farmers could not possibly reap many gains from them. Between 1930 and 1990, land under cultivation actually increased, but the number of farms declined from 6.5 to 2 million. Although Liberals reluctantly note this tendency, they do not understand that it has meant higher prices to consumers, with few, if any, benefits to most individually owned farms.

The market power of individual farmers, never very strong anyway, was eroded further during the 1950s and 1960s as marketing procedures were increasingly affected by the entrance of large business corporations into agriculture—*agribusiness*. Food chains bought orchards and feedlots and integrated their operations all the way from planting and slaughtering to the store checkout counter. Cereal producers, dairy products firms, baking companies, and other farm purchasers became more concentrated. At the same time, suppliers of farm machinery became increasingly integrated. As a result, farmers paid high, monopoly-established prices for equipment and had to sell their produce to comparatively few buyers. These buyers rarely had to pay more than the support price or "take it or leave it" prices for non-supported commodities. Contract production with big companies replaced the old market relationships. For instance, half of all fresh vegetables are grown under contract.

Meanwhile, agriculture also was being "discovered" by the large industrial conglomerates. Agribusiness grew and matured as ITT absorbed Wonder Bread and Smithfield Hams, Ling-Temco-Vought took control of Wilson Meats, Greyhound joined with Armour Packing, and other similar mergers took place. Basically, this phenomenon extended and accentuated the "price taker" situation of American farmers, even large farmers. Whether selling to the government, grocery chains, or General Foods, farmers had long been accustomed to dealing with buyers who set their own prices. The real power of this new and rejuvenated agribusiness, however, would be felt by the consumer as well. The new conglomerate middlemen in food production and distribution had the potential capacity to extract enormous profits. The structure for increasing food prices and middlemen's profits had been established. The only restraint was that posed by general overproduction in American agriculture. And the Russian grain deal soon changed that. By eliminating, for a few years at least, both the fact and the psychology of overproduction and comparatively low prices in agricultural goods, the deal paved the way for agribusiness to assert its power over table food prices.

In 1972, the United States and the Soviet Union secretly negotiated the sale of 19 million metric tons of American grain. Ironically, this sale was completed precisely as the United States was mining Haiphong harbor in North Vietnam and bombing rail lines north of Hanoi in an effort to stop the flow of Russian goods into the war zone. Although critics were to attack the sale as the "Great Grain Robbery," Secretary of Agriculture Earl Butz defended it as a boon to the American farmer. When accused of being willing to trade with the devil if it meant a profit, Butz replied, "If he has dollars."

The New Policy: A Failed Attempt to Keep Prices Up

The Russian grain deal of the 1970s, ancient history as it may seem to be, remains an important instructional example of how capitalism really works. Conventional economists love to talk about "the market" as if it were a perfectly neutral abstraction. The Russian grain deal puts the lie to that argument. The sale of American grain to the USSR actually reflected a highly calculated effort to create superprofits out of the anguish of farmers and the general public. Since the government itself lacked the legal authority to export goods, the grain sales had to be consummated by some half-dozen leading American grain-trading firms. The steps in the selling process were something like this: First, the harvest came in and could not be altered by farmer action. Second, the Department of Agriculture's Commodity Credit Corporation (CCC) granted the Russians exceptionally low credit arrangements. Third, the companies purchased the wheat owned and stored by the government in CCC bins and sold it to the Russians at a price significantly below the prevailing domestic price. Fourth, the companies, over and above their sales fees, received millions in subsidies from the government (the difference between the domestic price and the sale price).

The effects of the grain sales were injurious to practically all Americans except the grain companies and a few insiders who were able to make extraordinary profits by speculating on grain futures. Farmers were unable to take advantage of the resulting rise in wheat prices, since most had sold their grain to the government at the going market price. The American grain reserve was eliminated. Wheat prices and prices of substitute products went up, and so did the prices of beef and bread, both dependent on grain prices. Restive consumers were told it was just the law of supply and demand.

The Conservative prediction that growing world agricultural sales would eventually bring prosperity back to farming, although creating some hope in 1973 and 1974, had turned to ashes by 1978. Four years after Secretary Butz promised a new era for farming by opening American agriculture to the world, farmers had become dependent on world demand to get rid of two-thirds of their wheat, one-quarter of their corn, and half their soybeans. While American overseas grain sales remained fairly high, world grain prices (indeed, most world agricultural prices) tumbled.

And how did American consumers fare as agricultural prices fell? With large food corporations and agribusiness controlling the final goods prices for most U.S. food consumption, lowered per-unit farm prices meant higher profits, not lower prices at the grocery store. Food processors and distributors (who receive on the average 65 cents of every food dollar) saw their revenues and profits soar as farmers groaned and consumers cursed. Consumers blamed farmers. Farmers blamed unions for rising equipment costs and Arabs for higher energy and fertilizer bills. Almost no one placed the responsibility where it really belonged—with the grain-trading companies and their agents at the Department of Agriculture and with agribusiness monopolies, which were well represented in Washington.

What Strategy to Deal with the Problem?

From the Radical perspective, the farm problem has a number of different and troublesome dimensions. First of all, the chronic tendency toward overproduction and falling prices followed by underproduction and rising prices simply reflects the instability and irrationality of "free" markets. The vicious cycle that sometimes brings prosperity and sometimes crisis can be mitigated only by an effort to plan output and control prices. The trouble is that past control efforts have been biased toward helping the large farmer and agribusiness at the expense of the small farmer and the consumer. The share of government support payments going to giant enterprises has been growing. Farms with sales over $40,000 per year received 54 percent of all government payments in 1975. By 1995, they received 90 percent.

Such a payment schedule encourages increased production among the large farms while at the same time pushing the small producer to the wall. By and large, it has been the small and middle-sized farmers who are going broke, not the large farmers or farm corporations. In terms of our agricultural policy, that was precisely what was supposed to happen. Shifting the direction of payments toward smaller farmers would equalize income but also encourage inefficient farm producers to continue operations. The Gordian knot can be untied only if we develop an output and pricing program that humanely moves inefficient agricultural producers out of production while curbing the ability of the giant farm enterprises to set output and prices for their own—but not the consumer's—advantage.

Meanwhile, the development of policies regulating agribusiness and middleman processing profits is also essential. The tendency for food prices to remain high while farm prices fall can be explained only in terms of maintaining unjustified profits at the processing, transporting, or retail levels. Thus far, all farm policies—both Conservative market solutions and Liberal transfer payment systems—have avoided confronting a fact that every shopper knows: There is precious little correlation between periodically falling agricultural prices and the price of a market basket of food.

Yet, most Americans take eating for granted. Prices may affect our diets from time to time but most of us have little concern about the general availability of food. This is true even though probably not one in fifty of us has the slightest knowledge of how to grow the food we eat. And so it is, of course, that we are not inclined to think very deeply about our national agricultural policies. From a Radical perspective, this is a matter of considerable short-sightedness.

For Radicals, neither market-based policies nor Liberal intervention are very promising approaches to agricultural policy. While the exceptional productivity of American farmers is to be applauded, agriculture's propensity toward instability and its abiding submission to the needs and operational idiosyncrasies of corporate capitalism mean that, for all of us, the most essential of the essentials of life is beyond the reach of social control. For Radicals the fundamental irrationality of such a state of affairs is undeniably obvious.

Consumer Welfare

Is the Consumer Sovereign or Exploited?

Consumption is the sole end and the purpose of all production; and the interest of the producer ought to be attended to, only in so far as it may be necessary for promoting that of the consumer.

Adam Smith, 1776

The upshot of consumer protection, when it succeeds, is simply to hold industry to higher standards of excellence, and I can't see why they should object to that kind of incentive.

Ralph Nader, 1967

Let me emphasize: competition does not protect the consumer because businessmen are more softhearted than bureaucrats or because they are more altruistic or because they are more generous, but only because it is in the self-interest of the entrepreneur to protect the consumer.

Milton Friedman, 1978

Make no mistake: no one wants to roll the clock back on environmental, health, or safety regulations.

John F. Smith Jr., chairman, CEO, and president
General Motors Corporation, 1998

The Problem

Our survey of American agricultural policies illustrated the outcome of efforts to "correct" the market on behalf of certain producers of goods. We now turn to an example of market intervention on behalf of consumers. Just as we found that there is "no free lunch" when government acts to protect and promote certain sellers of goods, we now find that protecting buyers also exacts costs. While the existence of costs associated with such intervention is not a matter of much disagreement among economists and economic observers, there remains much disagreement on whether the costs are offset by direct benefits obtained.

For ordinary citizens, the consumer protection debate today plays a much smaller role in everyday economic concerns than it did fifteen to twenty years ago. However, it would be grossly inaccurate to infer from the comparative calm that the larger economic issues posed by consumer protection efforts have drifted into irrelevance.

According to the time-honored doctrine of *consumer sovereignty,* the final authority in determining production and prices is the consumer. In this view, consumers vote with their dollars in the marketplace. Their decisions are expressed by their final selection and willingness to pay for goods. In theory, at least, consumer sovereignty further presumes that buyers' tastes are given and unchanging, that buyers are expert and fully informed about products they are purchasing and the range of alternative products they might buy, and that prices are efficiently set in fully competitive markets. In the real world, however, such expectations, particularly those concerning buyer knowledge of the products they are purchasing, have long been viewed by many economists as unrealistic. As early as 1906, the federal government established the Pure Food and Drug Administration (which became the FDA) to protect consumers from adulterated food and unsafe drugs—two areas of consumer activity where acquiring the necessary knowledge to act "expertly" could in fact prove fatal. However, the development of a full-blown consumer protection movement is a comparatively recent phenomenon.

The consumerist movement was launched in 1965 with the publication of Ralph Nader's *Unsafe at Any Speed,* an effective muckraking attack on a popular General Motors car, the Corvair. Nader argued persuasively that the sporty rear-engined auto had a number of defects, among them a dangerous habit of flipping over when turning corners, even at low speeds. He also claimed that GM engineers and managers knew about the car's engineering deficiencies but had kept quiet about them. Corvair sales dropped after Nader's attack, although General Motors disputed his influence. The company made its last Corvair in 1969.

Spurred by Nader and his activists and by the sobering fact that auto fatalities had grown by about 1 percent each year since 1960, Congress enacted the National Traffic and Auto Safety Act in 1966. This legislation required that the auto industry begin to install certain specific safety features in all new cars. The first requirements (which went into effect in 1968) specified seat belts for all occupants, energy-absorbing steering columns, increased windshield resistance, dual braking systems, and padded instrument panels. Over the years, additional safety requirements have been mandated by the National Highway Safety and Traffic Safety Administration (also established in 1966).

Meanwhile, Nader's consumer advocate activities soon spread to other areas, and his popularity and political effectiveness grew. Within a few years, state and federal laws were introduced to give consumers greatly expanded power in product-liability and class-action suits. By 1975, over a million such suits were being initiated each year. More important, perhaps, was the creation of new consumer protection agencies. The Federal Trade Commission included a Bureau of Consumer Protection and a Bureau of Deceptive Practices. The executive branch boasted a special Assistant for Consumer Affairs and a Consumer Advisory Council. By 1980, more than 400 separate units in forty different government agencies were operating to advance consumer interests or protect consumer rights.

With the election of Ronald Reagan in 1980, the consumer protection movement began to lose momentum. Conservative Reagan had pledged to roll back government in all areas of economic life, and through the Reagan–Bush years (1981–1992) a series of administrative and budgetary decisions reduced the extent and intensity of consumer protectionist efforts by the federal government. Meanwhile, legislation was introduced (but not passed) that would have placed considerable restrictions on consumer-initiated product-liability suits.

Yet, at the end of the twentieth century, opinion surveys regularly show that most Americans still believe that an active consumer-protection effort by their government is proper public policy. Certainly the general popularity of the government's recent assault on the tobacco industry and the drift toward "criminalizing" smoking supports such a conclusion. Regardless of the economic consequences or the various contradictions involved, most citizens expect their government, at least to some degree, to "protect" them from the consequences of "consumer sovereignty."

Synopsis

Conservatives argue that consumers are best able to determine for themselves what they should buy and that efforts to "improve" on consumer rationality diminish satisfaction, raise prices, and lower economic efficiency. Liberals maintain that consumers do not have enough strength to protect themselves from the manipulative power of giant enterprises. Radicals go beyond mere "consumer protection," raising questions about the commitment of society to consume uncritically as an end in itself.

Anticipating the Arguments

- How do the Conservative, Liberal, and Radical views differ regarding the consumer's rationality and ability to choose freely and intelligently?
- In what ways do the Liberal and Conservative views of calculating the cost of goods differ?
- Why are Radicals suspicious of all efforts to "protect" consumers in a production-for-profit economic system?

THE CONSERVATIVE ARGUMENT

Consumer protection efforts exist in many guises. The earliest were at the turn of the century when a variety of state and federal laws aimed at maintaining the purity of food and drug products were passed. A second thrust developed in the 1930s with the passage of "disclosure legislation" that was intended to protect consumers from mislabeled or fraudulently labeled merchandise and false advertising. In the late 1960s and throughout the 1970s, consumer protectionism developed along a third line: specifying product standards for the alleged purpose of making all consumer products safer. Taken together, these three efforts, as they have developed over the past eighty years, constitute the contemporary American consumer protection movement.

Obviously, the consumer protection movement is neither a passing nor an inconsequential attempt by social engineers to "correct and improve on" the workings of the market. In fact, few efforts at market intervention have been so assiduously nourished as the belief that government is better able to protect and advance the interests of the consumer than anyone else—naturally enough, better than business, but even better than consumers themselves. Indeed, this idea sounds so sensible to many citizens that the irony of the last sentence will be lost entirely on many readers. However, in the name of consumer protection, consumers have been abused to a much greater extent than is generally appreciated.

Free Markets and the Freedom to Choose

To understand the Conservative position in the consumer protection debate, recall that all Conservative arguments start from the presumption that each individual's economic and political freedoms must be preserved—that free men and women making their own rational choices in the production and consumption of goods in free markets is the ideal social condition. While the exercise of individual freedom of choice may not always produce perfect economic and social consequences, "free" market conditions are ultimately preferable to those that arise in "regulated" or "protected" markets. Consequently, the underlying logic of Liberal consumer protectionists must be rejected out of hand since it rests on the view that individuals are not capable of making free choices affecting their own lives, or that if they do make such choices, there will be disastrous results. Such a dim view of people's abilities to reason and to choose, of course, inevitably leads to the conclusion that "more thoughtful" individuals must act to protect the ignorant majority. It is on such a rock of authoritarianism that Liberals build their arguments on behalf of social tinkering of all types, whether in the area of consumer affairs or in other realms of economic behavior.

Having said this, however, we must qualify our position in the case of consumer protection. Conservatives believe that sellers of goods, "free" though they may be, do not have the "right" individually or collectively to undertake conscious actions intended to do harm to consumers. Indeed, fraudulent sellers of shoddy products may be held responsible for damages resulting from their products, and damaged individuals must be able to recover losses resulting from fraudulent activities of sellers. Conservatives also recognize that the complexities of products present the modern consumer with problems in rationally evaluating and choosing among goods offered for sale. Consumers will be well served if a hidden hazard is brought to their attention either by the government or private agencies, so they can make purchases based on rational risk calculation, such as in the case of potential side effects of certain medicines. As Milton Friedman has accurately observed: "Insofar as the government has information not generally available about the merits or demerits of the items we ingest or activities we engage in, let it give us the information. But let it leave us to choose what chances we want to take with our own lives." Such a two-pronged effort on behalf of consumer protection goes a long way toward redressing the possible market imperfections that adversely affect consumers without destroying the market in the process. The freedoms of individual consumers to choose from among a broad range of alternative goods will not be impaired, as they invariably are under a Liberal "protectionist" scenario. The Conservative solution also avoids the peculiar "unfreedom" that excessive consumer protectionism ultimately produces. After all, it takes little imagination to see that government efforts to insulate us from all risks associated with goods we might voluntarily choose to consume must require the elimination of a wide range of useful or pleasurable goods—from stepladders to bicycles—that even in their ordinary use might cause us harm.

The High Cost of Safety

Simple and rational as the Conservative proposal is, it has not been the strategy we have adopted as a nation. Over the past eight decades or more, Americans have come to accept the philosophy and practices of an ever-growing body of consumer protection legislation, apparently on the premise that more protection will lead to fuller, more satisfied lives. The premise, however, fails on a number of grounds. The level of consumer protection we have been drifting toward imposes very heavy costs not fully appreciated by consumers. The costs of protection are levied in two ways. First, as taxpayers we must absorb the administrative overhead of operating numerous consumer protection agencies.

A second cost burden, and one of monumentally greater proportions, is the higher price of products, caused by the increased production costs that consumer protection efforts produce. For instance, the Consumer Product Safety Commission (CPSC), with jurisdiction over 10,000 products, requires manufacturers to keep detailed records on the performance of all products and even more substantial records of testing and evaluation on any product that may be deemed to "create a substantial risk of injury"—a category that has come to include everything from power mowers and stepladders to bathrobes and infant back-carriers. The CPSC also has the power to recall products, demand their redesign, and, ultimately, to ban them altogether. All these costs are absorbed by the manufacturer. To these costs, arising in extreme but not uncommon cases, firms must add the ordinary costs of keeping abreast of the blizzard of CPSC paperwork and hiring professional "safety experts," recall managers, public relations specialists, and the like. Of course these business costs are then passed along to consumers. Incidentally, these costs may be spread among a whole array of a firm's products; consequently, certain products not directly affected by consumer protection activities or made safer by protection may actually bear some of the protection costs associated with other goods.

How large the final bill is for consumers is uncertain, but one study of auto safety requirements legislated between 1968 and 1982 placed direct costs at about 10 percent of manufacturers' total costs (and this does not count another 13 percent of production costs required to cover mandated environmental protection measures).

Is It Worth It? The Cost-Benefit Question

The conventional Liberal justification for the high and escalating costs of consumer protection rests on *cost-benefit analysis.* According to this method of accounting, protectionist endeavors can be undertaken as long as the net money amount of social gains or benefits, after subtracting all private and social costs resulting from such requirements, continues to grow. (Or, to put it in the stricter terms of economic jargon, up to the point where marginal social costs equal marginal social benefits.) Nowhere has this technique of calculating the gain from required safety been so extensively applied as in auto safety. Needless to say, the protectionist advocates have been able to prove to their own satisfaction that the money value of safety costs are but a small fraction of the money value of social gains obtained from safety requirements. Unless the calculating techniques are examined closely, cost-benefit arguments are impressive. For instance, a 16–to-1 benefit-to-cost ratio was reported by the National Highway Safety Administration for one improved standard for auto windshields. Sounds impressive, right?

The key, however, to any cost-benefit analysis is the calculation of benefits. Benefits, of course, are equal to private and social outlays that would have to be made if the degree of protection required *was not* required. Naturally, benefits look impressive when lost earnings, property damage, medical costs, and the like, attributable to a presumably preventable hazard, are estimated quite high and less impressive if lower estimates are applied. But here is the problem with calculating benefits. Benefit estimation is certainly not an exact science and the estimator's efforts are usually self-serving. Thus it is no surprise that the government agency, the U.S. Safety Administration, sets the overall cost of auto accidents three times higher than the cost calculated by the private National Safety Council. The higher estimate increases the justification for greater auto safety requirements since larger benefits (in terms of reduced personal and social losses) will accrue.

Calculation of benefits is not the only difficulty. Costs are a sticky issue too. Each mandated safety cost is an *opportunity cost*—dollars not spent in some other way. For instance, what if the billions of dollars spent by automakers to meet safety standards (and presumably passed on to auto buyers) were spent on driver education? Would the social benefits be greater or less? No one really knows—most certainly not the Liberals who use cost-benefit analysis to justify, rather than to objectively evaluate, consumer safety actions.

For Conservatives, quite apart from the challenge of calculating social costs and benefits, cost-benefit analysis fails for more fundamental reasons. It simply defies the logic of the free market, replacing it with political value judgments. Accordingly, the cost-benefit method is inefficient and unfair. Individuals, rather than purchasing units of "safety" according to their preferences and willingness to pay, are obligated to pay for safety they do not want. Rational suburbanites who keep their fingers out of their lawn mowers must pay for protection devices they don't need. Although mental midgets who might, out of perverse curiosity, put a finger into the mower blades are protected (thus providing some alleged social gain), the thoughtful operator who gains nothing must pay more. In effect, efforts to obtain an uncertain, elusive degree of greater social benefits require that private cost-benefit considerations—the very heart of free markets in operation—be disregarded.

The search for greater net social benefits may actually produce the opposite—people acting against their own interests. For instance, higher-priced but safer cars may force some consumers to drive older, unsafer ones. But, most important, such an approach toward consumers attacks the fundamental freedom of choice and therefore compromises the liberty—even the liberty to act foolishly—that Conservatives consider so essential to a free society and a free economy.

THE LIBERAL ARGUMENT

The Classical economic assumption—that buyers and sellers bargain equally in the marketplace and that buyers, acting with restraint and wisdom, are sovereign—falls into the same intellectual category as belief that the world is flat. As in the case of the "flat worlders," a great many compelling reasons can be mustered to "prove" the argument, but they fly in the face of virtually all available evidence.

The Need for Intervention

From the Liberal viewpoint, protectionist interference in the private production of goods is justifiable and necessary for several reasons. First and foremost is the fact that as products have become more complex, they present potential risks and hazards that consumers are simply unprepared to evaluate and act on rationally. Sometimes the effects are comparatively benign; for example, the consumer buys a product that fails to function as promised in its advertising and labeling, and the only loss is the purchase price. But sometimes the product is dangerous and the consumer has no way of knowing this. Without government intervention, how would we have learned about the dangers of thalidomide, red dye no. 2, tris, cyclamates, certain pesticides, and other commodities that have been removed from the market for health reasons?

Second is the matter of *external costs*—costs paid by society that may not be accounted for in the selling price of a good. Consider the case of the automobile. Conservatives would look at only the private cost of an automobile: how much an individual must pay in the marketplace for a minimally equipped transportation vehicle. Additional costs for safety features are seen as purely private purchasing decisions: Buy safety if *you* want it. This misses an important point in understanding real costs. Automobiles have a cost that goes beyond merely the production, assembly, and sales expenditures and the expected profits of the automaker. The private decision to drive an unsafe but cheaper car means that society pays an additional bill for the costs inflicted on others by automobile accidents. Auto accidents, however, affect more people than just those who are injured. They lead to higher insurance rates, greater court costs, and heavier expenditures on roads, accident prevention, and enforcement. Nor are injuries or deaths simply "personal" matters. These human losses mean the dollar loss of present wage earnings and the loss of productive workers (now and in the future) and thus a greatly expanded social cost to the whole society.

Thus the Conservatives' argument against safety standards on the ground that they unfairly raise consumer costs is misguided. Higher-priced autos, and many other commodities, are necessary to cover all the costs certain goods generate. As we shall see, it is still a good bargain.

Restraining Sellers

The extraordinary growth of giant enterprises over the past century, along with the development of huge advertising budgets and sophisticated selling techniques, has created immense power on the sellers' side of the market. Economic concentration has given producers great freedom in establishing and maintaining their own price and quality standards. Mass advertising, meanwhile, has moved well beyond an informational function to one of actually creating and manipulating consumer wants. In such a situation, it is essential that government intervene on behalf of consumers to protect them from false advertising and poorly made or dangerous merchandise.

The efforts in the 1970s in automobile safety demonstrate how governmentally supported consumer protection actions can improve the quality of an important consumer good. Besides a house, a car is usually the largest single purchase made by a consumer. Americans own about 160 million cars. Once considered a rich man's luxury (and, after the Model T, the poor man's luxury), today the auto has become everyone's necessity. The vast majority of citizens are dependent on the auto to get to work, school, stores, and many recreational activities.

However, just as consumers began to buy more and more cars after World War II, automakers began to shift consumer attention from a car's serviceability and economy to its size, horsepower, and styling. (This trend actually had begun with General Motors in the early 1930s, but depression, war, and poor highways did not allow it to blossom until the late 1940s and 1950s.) The "ideal" car became one with speed, internal comfort, and annual style changes that could quickly distinguish it from last year's model or from other manufacturers' offerings. While social critics sneered at Americans' fancies and fantasies in automobiles, very few paid much attention to safety hazards. Autos had probably never been very safe, but by 1965, about 55,000 Americans were dying each year on the roads. New highways, along with greater horsepower and more weight, had made automobiles lethal weapons. The auto industry, which had shrunk from ten producers to just four, paid no attention to safety standards. Their advertising and research emphasized speed and comfort, and the buying public had accepted these values. Until Ralph Nader and a few others focused attention on safety inadequacies, rarely did car dealers have to respond to queries about how safe their products were.

Since the 1970s, all this has changed. Government, working through Congress and protection agencies (such as the National Highway Safety Administration), created minimum safety requirements for all cars: safety belts, bumper improvements, window defrosters, stronger glass, and the like. Careful monitoring of autos has led to massive recalls to remedy specific safety deficiencies. And, of course, the CPSC's and FDA's monitoring in other product areas have similarly contributed to the improvement of product quality and consumer safety throughout the economy.

The Savings from Safety

Government safety requirements have no doubt added to the price of what we buy, although much less than Conservatives have argued.

Safety belts, for instance, which (when used) have radically reduced serious injuries in collisions, add less than 1 percent to the price of a $20,000 automobile. The problem, of course, is to measure the increases in costs to consumers against the savings to society from reduced auto hazards. It would be inaccurate to stress only increased auto prices in a survey of auto safety costs and benefits.

Literally dozens of cost-benefit studies have been undertaken since the early 1970s in an effort to compare actual costs paid by the consuming public for auto safety devices and the actual benefits thereby obtained. No reasonably thoughtful study has ever demonstrated that the aggregate private safety costs exceed the aggregate social and private safety benefits obtained. Practically all studies indicate that a dollar in safety outlays produces at least two dollars in benefits, with most showing a vastly larger ratio of benefits to costs. The benefits are measured principally by calculating the reductions in lifetime or short-term earnings and associated medical costs that would have been lost in auto fatalities and injuries but were saved by the employment of auto safety devices. To these actual dollar losses, we could also add— if a figure were actually calculable—the value derived from the psychological satisfaction a driver or rider obtains from knowing (even if they are never involved in an accident) that theirs is a safer automobile.

To say, as Conservatives do, that such a cost-benefit argument is Liberal "hooey" is nonsense. Proof of that fact can be discovered by looking at one's own auto insurance policy. Quite simply, insurers would not provide the specific premium discounts they do for optional safety items if such items did not in fact reduce injury claims against the insurer.

Meanwhile, manufacturers complain that enforced recalls of cars to remedy defects constitutes an assault on their profits, and there is probably some truth to this. The answer, however, is better workmanship and engineering on the industry's part, not relaxed consumer protection. The cost for shoddy construction must be borne by industry, not by society at large.

If there is any serious defect in the government's efforts to protect consumers, it is that not enough has been done. The Highway Safety Bureau, for instance, operates on a yearly budget of about $150 million and employs a staff of about 1,000. That is a very small bureaucracy indeed to watch over safety standards in the nation's largest consumer-oriented industry.

The recent trend toward deregulation and reducing government interference in business decision making will cost the nation dearly if it
continues. Conservatives are right in saying that withdrawing safety and
consumer protection standards (and environmental and job safety standards as well) could lead to lower-priced goods or, more realistically,
greater industry profits. But these are cruel and false gains obtained
only through "creative accounting"—by shifting the social or external
cost of goods onto certain groups in the society. Greater efforts in
consumer safety are essential. Consumer protection will not be attained
until *caveat emptor* (let the buyer beware) is replaced by *caveat venditor* (let the seller beware) as the dominant motto of the marketplace.

THE RADICAL ARGUMENT

The relevant issues in the controversy over improved consumer safety
are rarely raised. Conservatives approach the question as a matter of
maintaining free markets and free choice, and Liberals argue for the
improvement of market conditions and the protection of buyers; but
these are really evasions of what the consumer safety question high-
lights. Why, in an advanced and supposedly civilized society such as
ours, is consumer safety a problem at all? Is it that we lack the resources and technology to manufacture safe products? On the contrary,
we all know that technology has nothing to do with the problem.
Unsafe autos, like unsafe food and dangerous drugs, are just "there."
They are part of our economic and social systems—to be tolerated or,
when things get bad enough, to be reformed. They are the necessary
but unwanted effects of an irrational social order.

Why "Consumer Sovereignty" Doesn't Exist

Capitalist economic systems are organized to make profits, not to make
people happy or to make life safer. For a capitalist enterprise to make
large profits, it has to sell in great quantity, and must obtain as great a
surplus over costs as possible. Obviously that calculation nowhere con-
tains any estimate of social costs and benefits. Insofar as the production-for-profit system is concerned, satisfaction is maximized simply if
we have *more*. Irrespective of the time-honored tradition of consumer
sovereignty, it is not really the consumers' power to choose among
goods that is important. What is important is that they consume, pe-

riod. Citizens in a capitalist society are taught from birth to accept uncritically that the object of life is to obtain goods; the more goods, the better their lives.

Looked at this way, it is easy to see why modern capitalism periodically becomes absorbed in such developments as the consumer protection issue. The social costs of the mass consumption of dangerous products as well as private concerns about safety have finally developed to such a point where reformist action must be taken. The recent auto safety movement, for instance, is merely another step in the long progression of product reform movements. It differs very little from the public outcry against adulterated food that created the Food and Drug Administration in 1906. The FDA certainly improved food cleanliness, just as the modern consumer movement has made cars safer to drive (or at least we all believe so). However, the "success" of such reforms deflects us from questioning the reasonableness of an economic system that sells poisoned food or hazardous vehicles in the first place.

Conservatives and Liberals may bicker over whether consumer sovereignty is best expressed in free or regulated markets, but both are committed to encouraging high levels of essentially irrational consumption. No traditional economist has ever proposed that consumer sovereignty be defined as the rational, coordinated control of production by the users of goods. That, of course, would lead to the abolition of the capitalist system. However strongly Conservatives and Liberals seem to disagree on the extent of government interference with production, both hold firmly to the principle of maintaining high levels of output as well as the primary goal of production for profit.

The Self-Serving Use of the Safety Idea

Americans have been misled about the high costs of safety. Conservatives emphasize that safety features increase product prices. Liberals admit that price increases are an outcome but that the costs are worth it given the social benefits obtained. The thrust of both arguments is that safety costs money—and corporations have not missed their cue. With a public prepared by the media and the economics profession to accept higher prices as the cost of greater protection, business has used the safety argument to push prices even higher. Back in 1977, as extensive safety requirements were being built into American autos, General

Motors reported a record-breaking net income of $4 billion on sales of $55 billion. At the same time, this firm, supposedly racked by the costs of expensive safety features, managed to rank thirty-seventh among the top 500 American corporations in income as a percentage of shareholders' equity. And paid earnings-per-share were two-thirds higher than stockholder earnings a decade earlier, in pre-consumerist 1966. Ford and Chrysler also ranked in 1977 in the top 200 firms in earnings ratio, with their earnings-per-share record better than a decade earlier (Ford's had increased almost 100 percent). Such evidence seems to suggest that, initially at least, the safety boom of the 1970s may have been a ploy for digging even deeper into consumers' pockets and, of course, hiding the action.

Only later, as the economy stagnated in the late 1970s and early 1980s, did corporate management begin to push energetically against many previously accepted safety mandates. Faced with declining domestic demand and rising imports of foreign-made products, it became expedient to use "safety costs" as a contributing factor in the profit squeeze felt by many American firms. In the auto industry especially, consumer, environmental, and job safety programs *and* workers' salaries were obvious targets. Automakers quickly mounted a highly successful public relations and political lobbying effort to "take back" on all these fronts. Once a boon to profit making, auto safety was now depicted as a threat to profits as well as to the continued strength of a basic American industry. In the new political and economic setting, many consumers even became convinced that we could no longer afford rigorous auto safety standards.

The Radical Dilemma

No doubt the Radical position seems hopelessly negativistic and irrelevant to the specific question of "protecting the consumer"; indeed it is if Radicals are expected by conventional economists to offer long-run remedies that do not consider the underlying philosophy and social organization of consumption activities in a capitalist society. Radicals understand that capitalism is propelled by the private search for profit and that profits increase, *ceteris paribus,* either by increasing sales or by keeping costs down. Profits by themselves are not tied to intrinsic social concerns about safety—unless, of course, "safety" can be used as a gimmick to raise prices. Similarly, Radicals understand that Liberal efforts to improve product safety, regardless of their posturing on behalf of consumers, cannot seriously assault the profit prerogatives or the rights of capitalists in a production-for-profit economy. Liberal actions on behalf of the abused in a production-for-profit system can never be so massive that they damage the basic system.

Given the constraints of a system that depends on private profit-making on the one hand, and, on the other, requires the political pretense of repairing the more egregious functional shortcomings and social atrocities resulting from such a system, Radicals are inclined to ask a broader philosophical question: *Why don't we have a more rational approach toward the production and use of goods?* Conservatives adroitly avoid raising the issue of how demand may be manipulated by advertising, and Liberals pay little more than lip service to this problem. Both fail to understand how a "consumer society" may become locked into thoroughly irrational patterns of consumption. However, if we see that most purchases are made because the goods are merely being sold, rather than because we have received cerebral messages that we *need* the particular commodities, it will become easier to unravel the dilemma of wasteful consumption as well as the consumption of unsafe products.

Of course, people shouldn't have to drive unsafe cars, nor should they have to own unsafe "pet rocks" or any other item sold in a capitalist society. Neither should automakers (or even pet rock sellers) be able to profit from selling "safe" automobiles (or "safe" pet rocks). For Radicals, however, the issue is really whether the goods themselves are socially useful. It is not a matter of making socially wasteful goods "safe." The Radical, then, approaches the question of consumer welfare by questioning the very goods that are offered for sale. For instance, in the case of the privately owned automobile and the enormously expensive system of roads and ancillary services needed to make auto ownership feasible, most Radicals see an incredibly irrational and wasteful transportation mode. Accordingly, Radicals view the debate over private automobile safety and the virtual absence of any discussion about devising an efficient system of mass transportation as a good example of how we never address the basic questions in our analysis of consumer behavior.

However, recognizing that the broader questions of "what and why we consume" are not part of the present economic agenda, Radicals, in addressing the current consumer protection problem concretely, embrace most protectionist objectives: the maintenance of quality and purity in product manufacture, the accurate dissemination of information about a product's uses and limits, the recall of dangerous products, and the ability of the consumer to gain redress for damages and defrauding. *Caveat venditor* is an acceptable short-term strategy, but it scarcely goes to the root of our problems as long as production-for-profit drives the nation's economic and political engine.

Dealing with Externalities
How Can We Save the Environment?

These pollutants originate in the Midwest, eastern Canada, and western New York State; rain and snow wash them out of air passing over the state [of New York] to fall on our forests, lakes, and cities. Because some of these air pollutants become sulphuric acid, nitric acid, and other acids when dissolved in the precipitation carrying them to earth, this whole process has been dubbed "acid rain."

John Hawley, The Conservationist, *1977*

Are we going to have to count bodies before we determine that the time has come to reduce sulfur emissions throughout the whole country to ensure there is no impact on human health? . . . We don't need more evidence to conclude that action needs to be taken.

Dr. David Axelrod, New York State
Health Commissioner, 1984

When we calculate all the costs to everyone, on balance, we will save money when we pass this [the Clean Air] bill.

Senator George Mitchell, 1990

You don't have to be a scientist to know it's been dangerously hot this summer.

Vice President Al Gore, 1998

The Problem

They began to notice the problem in the Adirondack Mountains of upstate New York over two decades ago. Plant and aquatic life in many of the region's lakes began to undergo a significant change reflecting a general degradation of lake water quality. Within a few years the problem rapidly worsened as dozens of lakes became "dead"—virtually void of fish and plants. The cause, at least as far as New Yorkers were concerned, was "acid rain." Precipitation containing high levels of sulfuric acid and other acids was altering nature's balance, not only killing lakes but showing signs of damaging the trees and ground cover as well. The source of the acid rain was, to most scientists, easily explained: The burning of fossil fuels unleashed sulfur dioxide, nitrogen dioxide, and other chemicals and particulates into the atmosphere. These returned to earth with falling rain and snow and, combined with water, became highly acidic. Since northern New York had no significant fossil fuel burning, the source of the problem was determined to be the industrial Midwest. There, manufacturing plants and electric generating facilities belched large quantities of chemicals into the air from high smokestacks, to be carried northeastward and deposited by the prevailing wind and weather systems.

In general terms, at least, economic theory offers both a theoretical explanation and a potential remedy to the problems posed by acid rain and other types of environmental pollution. The theoretical tool employed is the concept of "externalities." The analysis runs like this: Under free market conditions, the interaction of all individual sellers (supply) and all individual buyers (demand) establishes a market price for a product. Yet the market price may not reflect all the incidental costs or benefits associated with the good. For instance, a student may value (in terms of his or her estimated private benefits) a college education at around $70,000 or $80,000, but society in general may derive benefits of much greater value from individuals who obtain college educations. A better-educated public may be more creative, more efficient, and harder-working, thus producing a larger economic pie for everyone, not just the solitary student. These additional gains are spillover or external *benefits* (sometimes called *external economies*) beyond the actual market price paid for the commodity.

In the case of acid rain or pollution, however, we are talking about spillover or external costs (also known as *external diseconomies*). In a market economy, output decisions are based on calculations of direct production costs. Air, water, and even the land space itself may be viewed as "free goods" in the production process. Insofar as the atmosphere and the earth are "free" sewers and dumping grounds, the producer enjoys a private benefit by polluting. Society, living in a dirtier world, however, accumulates social costs. The market price of the good is obtained by not internalizing the social costs into the costs of manufacturing the good. Obviously, to be efficient in its production and pricing decisions, an economy needs to calculate all costs, both private direct production costs and social costs, in setting a price for a good. The objective of an efficient economic policy, then, is to internalize the social costs of pollution in the price of the good so that preventive or remedial action may be paid for.

However, the step from theory to practice is a big one. From the viewpoint of New Yorkers (and New Englanders and Canadians, too, who have been living with acid rain for some time), it is essential to attack acid rain at its source by restricting midwestern industrial emissions. At the same time, naturally enough, midwesterners have an interest in keeping their industries operating at low costs and in obtaining cheap steam-electric energy.

Maintaining environmental quality has been a highly popular social priority with Americans for more than three decades, but acid rain has been a tough problem. Unlike most pollution, which affects the immediate surroundings of the polluter and usually inspires community pressure on the polluter, acid rain's apparent source and its effects are a thousand miles and many state lines separated from one another. Given conflicting regional interests, it is difficult to comprehend any solution to the acid rain problem below the federal level. Moreover, any resolution at that level would require, both in scope and application, a much broader application of the Environmental Protection Agency's powers than has been exercised to date. But beyond the politics of maintaining environmental safeguards, there remain important economic questions. How, precisely, does one determine the social cost of acid rain? How is its source to be pinpointed? And even if the cost and the specific polluters are identified, what means should be undertaken to internalize the social cost?

Conservatives, Liberals, and Radicals come to quite different policy conclusions in answering these three questions, even when they start from an agreement about acid rain's existence, its threat, and its source. The issue, of course, is not simply acid rain but a strategy that will be effective in dealing with all environmental problems.

Synopsis

Conservatives recognize the "neighborhood effects" of pollution and advocate a cost-benefit technique in determining the amount of environmental cleanup outlays. They favor use of emissions taxes, operating through the market mechanism itself, as the best way to allocate cleanup costs. Liberals place less trust in market-based tax schemes and favor direct government controls or even the use of a subsidy policy to clean up the environment. Radicals argue that most efforts to protect the environment are doomed to failure since actual environmental damage is always underestimated. Production-for-profit systems simply do not find it to their advantage to undertake truly effective actions to protect the environment.

Anticipating the Arguments

- On what grounds do Conservatives favor emissions taxes over direct government controls in eliminating pollution?
- On what grounds do Liberals believe that emissions taxes are insufficient in dealing with pollution problems?
- Why do Radicals believe that conventional market-directed or government-directed efforts are likely to be insufficient in protecting the environment?

THE CONSERVATIVE ARGUMENT

The debate over pollution and acid rain raises a somewhat different set of economic and theoretical questions from those considered in our earlier discussion of automobile safety. Owning and wearing seat belts is (or at least should be) a purely voluntary matter directly affecting no one but the party involved. Pollution, on the other hand, focuses directly on third-party effects—damage done to individuals who have no economic stake in the polluting action and who can exercise no voluntary control over the effects of pollution.

According to Milton Friedman and most others who have looked at the pollution issue, there is a "neighborhood effect" that must be calculated and accounted for. According to Friedman:

> A ... general class of cases in which strictly voluntary exchange is impossible arises when actions of individuals have effects on other individuals for which it is not feasible to charge or recompense them. This is the problem of "neighborhood effects." An obvious example is the pollution of a stream. The man who pollutes a stream is in effect forcing others to exchange good water for bad. These others might be willing to make the exchange at a price. But it is not feasible for them, acting individually, to avoid the exchange or to enforce appropriate compensation.*

Neighborhood Effects and the Role of Government

Clearly in this situation, it is appropriate to expect the community to establish some technique for determining the costs that one individual imposes on another and to develop a mechanism for allocating the costs. Admitting to such occasional needs to remedy market failures, however, should not be construed as a total condemnation of the market or as license to introduce all manner of "benevolent" tinkering with the market. Indeed, it becomes quite important that the community action chosen to deal with neighborhood effects be as neutral and nonbureaucratic as possible. Quite simply, the object is to develop a policy that makes a firm internalize all of its costs (social as well as private) in its production decisions.

In our time, magnificent government structures have been created in the name of protecting the innocent from the polluters. Yet society's gains from expensive and creative antipollution efforts have been

---

*Milton Friedman, *Capitalism and Freedom* (Chicago: University of Chicago Press, 1962), p. 30.

few—and often obtained only at an unacceptable burden to everyone's voluntary rights and to economic well-being and efficiency in general. Consider the ruthless application of antipollution standards in the 1970s. With the creation of the Environmental Protection Agency (EPA) in 1970 and the passage of the Clean Air Act in the same year, the EPA was given authority to (1) determine national air quality standards; (2) set emission levels for old and new plants; (3) set motor vehicle emission standards; (4) establish which fuel substances may be burned in motor vehicles; and (5) establish standards in emergency situations (including the power to close down industrial polluters presenting an "immediate danger" to public health).

With great zeal and little contemplation of the consequences, the EPA wrote standards and enforced them vigorously. Murray Weidenbaum of the Center for the Study of American Business has estimated that between 1979 and 1986, public agencies and private firms spent nearly three-quarters of a trillion dollars in efforts to meet the EPA requirements. Looking at the data another way, Weidenbaum estimates that meeting EPA direct control standards absorbed 14 percent of the paper industry's capital outlays and 20 percent of the steel industry's new investment. Before the Reagan administration began to relax EPA direct pollution controls in the early 1980s, nearly 200 plants employing over 200,000 workers had closed as the direct result of imposed pollution abatement costs.

Did such antipollution costs produce benefits? The answer is a qualified yes. National urban air quality has improved fairly steadily since 1974. The Great Lakes and the Far West have experienced significant environmental improvements. The expected national rate of environmental damage that would have occurred without pollution controls has slowed, with actual damages falling in recent years. However, it is a matter of some debate whether the benefits, in dollar terms, came anywhere close to the dollar costs imposed by the EPA.

The problem in dealing with acid rain and other pollution problems lies in establishing a method for bringing costs of control and benefits into balance. It is patent nonsense to argue as Radicals and some Liberals do that an absolutely clean environment is essential *whatever its cost*. To begin with, there is no technically feasible way to return the environment to its unspoiled, pre-fossil-fuel-era standards regardless of the cleanup outlays we might undertake. We shall be left always with some level of environmental damage.

Given this fact, we must establish reasonable cleanup expectations that are based on (1) the value of real benefits actually attainable and (2) the community's willingness to pay the cost of obtaining such benefits. Government-imposed cleanup costs vastly in excess of antipollution benefits that the community deems reasonable lead to a serious misallocation of resources, resulting in closed plants, inadequate new capital investment, failing world competitiveness, lost jobs, and other consequences.

The techniques available for determining reasonable cleanup objectives and bringing the costs into balance with the benefits are various. From a Conservative perspective, the most useful techniques employ the minimum of social tinkering and the greatest reliance on forces of the market to bring social and private benefits into line with social and private costs.

The Possibility of Private Approaches

Although reliance on the market to deal with neighborhood effects has its limitations, two private (nongovernment) means of assigning the costs of pollution to polluters are possible: negotiation among affected parties and setting specific liability rules. Although their effectiveness is limited, they deserve mention.

Negotiation of pollution costs between polluters and damaged parties is feasible where one person's property rights are clearly damaged by a second party's polluting—for instance, a city's loss of its water supply or added costs in preparing its drinking water because of a single identifiable upstream polluter. Given recourse to the courts, the damaged party may sue for damages, which gives an incentive to the polluter to clean up its emissions. In fact, the polluter and the damaged party may sit down and bargain rather than go to court. Presumably, the pollution fee or the extent of cleanup agreed to reflects both parties' balancing of benefits and costs.

Failing negotiation, liability rules depend on use of the courts to establish private costs resulting from pollution. Once the court sets particular damages for polluting actions, the firm must calculate such damages as a fairly certain cost of any production having polluting side effects. If the firm pollutes more, it pays more; if it pollutes less, it pays less. The incentive—without any government directives—is on the side of reducing pollution.

The obvious difficulty with relying on negotiations and liability rules is that they don't work well when the specific effects of a specific polluter are uncertain or where specifically damaged parties are either hard to determine or have difficulty establishing clear property rights. How, in fact, does a New York fisherman establish the level of personal damage from acid rain and determine who actually caused the acidity in the first place?

Collective Action

Given the shortcomings of purely private approaches to environmental issues, we are left with collective action as the only alternative. Collective action comes in only three general forms: direct controls, emissions taxes or permits, and subsidies.

Conservative opposition to direct controls was already noted. When government sets specific emissions standards backed with the force of fines or the power to close plants, government wields a dangerous degree of power. Even if used cautiously, there is no certainty that this power will produce the desired effect of balancing cleanup costs and benefits. As a matter of practice, government has tended to overvalue the benefits of halting or slowing pollution while underestimating the costs of attainment. To a considerable degree, direct controls reflect imperfect pollution-measuring standards that vary widely from firm to firm, industry to industry, and region to region.

Most important, however, direct controls provide little monetary incentive for the marginal polluter (at or just below the accepted emission standard) to reduce pollution at all. Direct controls can, at best, establish only an acceptable minimum; they have no effect in bringing about a generally improving environmental quality as a function of a market economy's constant drive to lower costs.

Subsidies paid to firms as inducements to installing antipollution devices may sound attractive but are hopelessly inefficient. Like direct emissions controls, there is a strong element of imposed government problem solving that looks better than it really is. Subsidies provide no market-based inducement for firms to take antipollution actions; they do not cause firms to internalize the social costs of polluting. Ironically, they simply lower polluters' costs, possibly increasing levels of pollution in the long run. If government installed "scrubbers" in the smokestacks of midwestern coal-burning plants, which are allegedly the source of acid rain, the effect would be to lower production costs (in terms of the alternative of the firm's internalizing its own pollution costs). This might encourage more coal burning, wholly offsetting the initial clean air gains.

A more acceptable method for repairing the neighborhood effects of pollution is levying an emissions tax. The tax is essentially a levy on the firm equal to the amount of damage the particular firm is causing. Relying on the firm's desire to maximize profit, cleaning up its production emissions will lead to reductions in its pollution tax burden. Firms most able to adapt to antipollution requirements will respond most quickly, thus benefiting from the resultant tax reduction. Essentially inefficient or poorly managed enterprises that do not act to reduce emissions will find their profits adversely affected by the emissions tax.

Technical problems remain in metering the amount of an individual firm's emissions and translating this into a dollar value of social damages that will be the basis for estimating the tax. Nevertheless, the emissions tax concept is attractive because of its lack of direct intervention and its reliance on the firm's own profit-maximizing desires to make environmental protection work.

The question of how an emissions "charge" should best be levied remains a matter of some debate, but Conservatives favor the use of "marketable emissions permits." Under such an arrangement, a scientific determination of the environment's capacity to absorb pollutants over a given area would be determined. Then, pollution permits totaling the permissible annual volume would be auctioned off by a responsible public authority. Firms with high abatement costs (the costs of cleaning the air or water affected by their operations) would be inclined to pay higher prices for an emissions permit sold at auction. Those with low abatement costs might find it cheaper to do their own cleanup—as they would be required to do without acquisition of an emissions permit. Once issued, the permits will develop their own market, with firms buying and selling permits among themselves according to which is least expensive: paying their own abatement costs or buying a permit that allows a specified quantity of annual emissions from their manufacturing sites.

In either case, the environment is subjected to no more than a permissible level of toxic inputs. Government intervention is kept to a minimum. And everyone relies on market signals rather than social control in the everyday direction of resources toward a cleaner environment. This system avoids the inefficiency and inequity of direct controls.

Pitfalls Nevertheless

Though a feasible economic solution can be developed to deal with the problem of acid rain or pollution in general, technical problems should not be minimized. Metering emissions is still an imprecise science. Connecting emissions levels to specific damages (coal burning in Ohio to a dead lake in New York State) is still a matter of scientific debate. And determining the reasonable social valuation of a dead lake or stream (or revitalizing these bodies of water) on which any tax levy or penalty will be based is also a matter of much argument. We cannot return to the distant pristine past under any conditions, and determining the degree to which we want a "clean environment" must be done with the understanding that there is no such thing as a free lunch. Environmental quality improvements can come about only at a price.

THE LIBERAL ARGUMENT

Although Conservatives may seem reasonable enough in their concession that pollution involves neighborhood effects that the community has the right to regulate, their actual track record with regard to environmental protection is a poor one. Their less-than-enthusiastic embrace of federal government action to control pollution stems from their blind commitment to a "free market." Moreover, the pollution problem goes a long way toward demonstrating that free markets may not always ensure society's well-being.

The Failure of the Market to Allocate Externalities

As noted earlier, externalities arise when, beyond the market price of a good, there is either a calculable external cost (detrimental externality) or gain (beneficial externality) to the individuals consuming the good or to society as a whole. Externalities are not, as Conservatives might suggest, merely interesting exceptions to the theory of markets in which the free play of supply and demand establishes prices and allocates resources accordingly. Instead, they reflect a serious market failure and are ample justification for the Liberal assertion that "the market can very often be improved upon."

Externalities reveal two types of problems in allocating resources purely according to market dictates. First, there is the problem of external benefits or economies. A firm that perhaps inadvertently supplies substantial benefits to a community—say, by laying out attractive parklike playgrounds around its production site—has little monetary incentive to continue such investment in this site because it receives no gains in sales from such activity. Although the community derives esthetic and health benefits, there is no market incentive for the firm to allocate resources to such objectives (hence it is not surprising that most places of production are so drab). Second, whereas there is little incentive to invest in the "good things" that produce no private market gains, there is considerable incentive to spin certain costs off onto the community rather than internalize them as part of the firm's own production costs. Thus the rivers and the air have been viewed as free sewers by firms spewing chemicals out into the community, therefore not requiring the firm to invest in antipollution controls. Left to its own devices, a free market allocation of resources can be counted on to produce few beneficial externalities and many detrimental externalities.

In developing a useful economic policy, this logic of the market requires modification and redirection. In terms of our discussion of environmental problems posed by acid rain, we are addressing a specific problem that can only be dealt with through government action.

The Need for a National Environmental Policy

As a general rule, Conservatives oppose collective action, and in particular they oppose collective action at the federal level, preferring to support state and municipal intervention as more "democratically" responsive to local needs. Clearly, the case of acid rain demolishes such an argument. Ohio simply has no incentive to lower the acidity of New York's lakes. Hence Conservatives' first consideration for "voluntary" agreement between polluters and damaged parties is a flawed argument. Since New Yorkers possess few powers to persuade Ohioans to voluntarily reduce emissions, and since there is no economic advantage for the polluters to comply, negotiation between these distant and differently motivated parties is most unlikely.

Nor does the prospect of enforcing property rights and liability rules in the courts seem more probable. While class action suits against the polluters are technically possible, the legal system offers infinite delaying tactics. Moreover, individual damaged parties have no realistic possibility of financing these long legal battles against well-staffed and well-financed midwestern corporations.

Given the shortcomings of voluntarism and the interstate nature of the acid rain problem, it becomes quickly evident that only strong federal intervention provides a possible solution. Even the Conservative argument, despite basic opposition to broad collective action, concedes this point—at least theoretically. The Conservative political record nevertheless demonstrates a different view in practice. When it came to office in 1981, the Reagan administration, among its many efforts to reduce American society's commitment to providing collective goods and to offsetting externalities, undertook the destruction of the EPA (as it similarly began to erode the power of the Department of Education, the Department of Health and Social Services, and other government agencies). Administrators sympathetic to business (read: "polluters") needs began to wind down pollution control programs developed during the 1970s. "Superfund" cleanup programs ground to a halt, and no new efforts to exert federal leadership in cleaning up the environment emerged.

During the 1990s, the Republican-controlled Congress has continued the Reagan legacy of benign neglect. Whatever their arguments to the contrary, Conservatives have shown themselves markedly less concerned about neighborhood effects than maintaining corporate profits.

Direct Intervention Versus Emissions Taxes

Lately, emissions taxes and creating a market for emissions permits have become the rage among many economists. Supposedly by metering a firm's discharges and then taxing the firm on the basis of its measured pollution, a neutral tax mechanism develops that internalizes the external costs or diseconomies. The tax becomes another cost of production that the profit-maximizing firm will seek to lower by introducing emission controls. However, in the real world, things need not work this way at all. Technologically speaking, we are nowhere near the point where we can install pollution-measuring meters. Such methods simply do not exist. Thus we are not presently able to develop an effective pollution tax. And even with a tax in place, there is no certainty that firms will opt for less pollution rather than paying the tax. In many cases, paying the tax might be a less costly short-term strategy than undertaking the expense of removing pollutants from the air or water. Even in the most ideal scenario—efficient taxes and rational firms operating in competitive markets—emissions taxes are a slow process for forcing change in pollution habits.

Direct intervention, if seriously undertaken, promises a quicker short-run solution. By setting emission standards and enforcing them with stiff fines or the threat of plant closure, a firm has an immediate incentive to introduce emission controls. Should a carrot rather than a stick be preferred in inducing industry compliance with environmental standards, direct subsidies, either to pay for the cost of pollution control or as cash incentives to firms that voluntarily reduce emissions, could be paid.

The Conservative argument against direct controls and subsidies maintains that they are inefficient, creating greater total social and private costs than the value of the benefits obtained. This supposedly results from compelling too much antipollution activity too fast. Northeasterners, whose recreational areas are quickly deteriorating and whose water and forest resources face immediate danger from acid rain, are not likely to be impressed by such logic. While we may not be able to restore the environment to pre-Industrial-Era conditions, excessive cost consciousness may produce a "rational" pro-environment strategy that does nothing at all for the environment.

THE RADICAL ARGUMENT

Over the past three decades, a noteworthy social awareness has developed about various market failures and their effect on the quality of life under a capitalist system of production. With fairly substantial popular support in the 1970s, a number of collective efforts were launched to deal with such issues as consumer protection, occupational safety, developing new sources for energy and other scarce resources, and, of course, environmental protection. Yet two points are worth remembering: First, it was erroneously believed that more government intervention to correct any market failure was all that was needed. Second, the few timid gestures undertaken produced very limited benefits, and, in fact, we have recently marched away from the minor victories of the mid-1970s. The problem is that we have not seen "market failures" for what they really are: the market working precisely as it is supposed to work under a production-for-profit system.

Capitalism and the Environment

Profits, of course, are merely the revenues obtained by the capitalist after all production and distribution costs have been subtracted. To maximize profits, the rational capitalist must minimize costs. Insofar as it is cheaper (more profitable) to emit sulfur and other particulates into the atmosphere rather than invest in antipollution devices or nonpolluting production, acid rain and other environmental horrors are a quite "rational" and expected by-product of a production-for-profit system. Viewed this way, it becomes apparent that whatever the advantages to people in general from a clean environment, there are no advantages to a firm to undertake antipollution activities voluntarily. And this is also true of other socially directed objectives such as consumer protection and occupational safety.

The record of capitalist destruction of the earth, its atmosphere, and ultimately its inhabitants is obvious enough. The degradation of the land through clear-cutting hardwood timber in the nineteenth century to obtain nothing but tannic acid for bootmaking; the mid-twentieth-century practice of stripmining coal; the modern crises of acid rain and radioactive waste from a vast number of nuclear production sites illustrate that the search for private profits stands in open opposition to environmental, and hence human, concerns.

The Failure of Past Environmental Efforts

Liberals and Conservatives (who, after all, cannot deny the evidence of environmental decline) concede the need for some pro-environmental activity. Liberals tend to favor direct control mechanisms implemented by a benevolent and all-seeing state, whereas Conservatives prefer the use of neutral emissions taxes and marketable emissions permits that "induce" firms to reduce their polluting. Will either approach work?

The Liberal reliance on government direct controls or subsidies presumes, of course, that government is neutral—that government can determine environmental targets and develop and enforce rules that might directly threaten business enterprises' profits or continued operations. Yet the supposed neutrality of government in the marketplace has proved an illusive notion in practice. Even under Liberal administrations, the Environmental Protection Agency has shown a softness in forcing business to pay cleanup costs. Effectively using their lobbying power, firms have successfully pointed out that cleanup efforts that are too energetic can lead to lost profits, diminished ability to compete abroad, and finally to the loss of workers' jobs. In fact, even the unions have joined private enterprise in "going slow" on acid rain and other pollution problems. Accordingly, in the last years of the Carter administration, the EPA introduced "pollution offset" programs in which new firms and new plants could emit pollution so long as they could induce (pay) other firms to reduce emissions or within their own company reduce emissions elsewhere by an equal amount. Meanwhile, using a "bubble concept," old firms were given general permissible emissions limits over each plant, with the firm choosing where and how it cared to cut total pollution within the plant to meet the limits— more in the water and less in the air, or vice versa, if it was profitable. Such actions reflected concerns that too strenuous an antipollution policy could damage firm profitability. At best they slowed the rate of pollution buildup without recognizing the need to undo the crimes of the past as well as the present.

Conservatives showed their practical lack of concern for pollution problems during the Reagan–Bush years. While talk of emissions taxes and the sale of emission permits characterized the writings of Conservative economists when they actually addressed the pollution problem, no national emissions tax program was put in place. In fact, the EPA even pulled back from the limited level of effectiveness that characterized the Carter years. Meanwhile, although the avowedly Liberal administration of President Clinton has shown more interest in environmental problems and, occasionally, has shown more backbone in standing up to certain polluters, it has not produced a new and wide-ranging environmental effort.

To be perfectly blunt, even though surveys show that most Americans believe the environment must be protected "whatever the cost" and even though the public's environmental awareness is now well over three decades old, no effective national environmental program has emerged yet nor seems likely to emerge soon.

The Need to Get Beyond "Cost-Benefit"

For some, the Radicals' discounting of Liberal and Conservative environmental proposals will be interpreted as silly obstructionism. As in the case of consumer protection, the Radical opposition at first seems contradictory—that Radicals somehow oppose "serious" efforts to make safer products or to clean up the atmosphere. Such an inaccurate perception stems from a failure to grasp the basis of the Radical argument.

From a Radical perspective, failure to deal with environmental issues is not merely a capitalist oversight or some accidental consequence of a market-dominated society; it is directly traceable to capitalism's dominant feature—*the drive for profits*. Furthermore, it is not possible for capitalism to be itself (searching for profits) and to be better than itself (taking actions that reduce profits) at the same time. Capitalist (Conservative or Liberal) discussions about halting acid rain or cleaning up pollution in general are therefore nothing more than seductive deceptions.

The point becomes obvious when we peel back the Conservative and Liberal arguments to examine their real content. Both rely on a cost-benefit measurement of the extent of pollution as a problem and as an indicator of how much antipollution activity should be undertaken. The ultimate determinant of the extent of antipollution activity is, according to conventional theory, established by the point at which marginal social costs equal marginal social benefits (in other words, where the last dollar spent on cleaning up the environment is at least equal to a dollar's worth of gain from the actual cleanup). On the surface, this seems rational enough until we consider how costs and benefits are calculated. "Social costs" are seen as the sum of all private costs plus any governmental outlays for reducing pollution as determined by market-established prices. "Social benefits" are the sum of dollar benefits accruing to all individuals affected by the reduction of pollution. The bias of such an approach is always to overestimate costs and underestimate benefits, since costs are comparatively easily calculated in market terms while only a portion of benefits can be assigned a particular market value. A $10 million outlay for a steam electricity plant scrubber (whether paid for by the firm or by tax dollars) is easily perceived as a cost. However, what is the benefit of not killing a lake? A lake is only partly a commodity to which a market value can be assigned as a piece of real estate lost to its owners for personal or business use. A lake, a stream, or, more pointedly, a sunset has certain intrinsic values that are not calculable in current market terms.

Cost-benefit discussions under capitalism are always limited to property and commodity relationships. The "neighborhood effect" of Conservative theoreticians (and used also by Liberals) rests on calculating damages to individuals' property rights as the beginning point for offsetting spillover costs. Hence the estimated value of "social benefits"—which in discussions of external diseconomies are nothing more than the sum of estimable private property or market value gains—will always be stated lower than the real benefits to society of ending pollution.

In our previous discussion of consumer safety, we saw that once the issue was stripped to its basics, the conventional debate over consumer protection was off target and avoided the real issue of socially irrational production and consumption choices being the natural outcome of a production-for-profit system. As we found no remedy there to irrationality within even a modified capitalist system, we find no remedy forthcoming from efforts alleged to "offset" the market failure of external diseconomies resulting in acid rain or other pollution. Remedial antipollution actions of any consequence will take place only when social policies reflect real human needs, not the requirements and values of a commodity-dominated society. Ending pollution and maintaining a safe and humane environment, now and for the future, is a social goal that must be understood as having no ultimate "cost" limits with regard to what must be paid for its attainment. From a Radical perspective, society is more than the sum of each of its individual members. Society, or humankind, also has a historical dimension. We in the twentieth century have no right to limit the rights and blight the lives of human beings in the twenty-first century and beyond any more than midwesterners presently have the right to brew acid rain for northeasterners.

Imperfect Competition

What Should Our Policy Toward Big Business Be?

People of the same trade seldom meet together, even for merriment and diversion, but the conversation ends in a conspiracy against the public, or in some contrivance to raise prices.

Adam Smith, 1776

Every contract, combination in the form of trust or otherwise, or conspiracy, in restraint of trade or commerce . . . is hereby declared to be illegal. . . . Every person who shall monopolize, or attempt to monopolize, or combine or conspire . . . to monopolize . . . shall be deemed guilty of a misdemeanor.

Sherman Anti-Trust Act, 1890

The problem in American is not that the top 100 corporation presidents are violating the laws, though God knows they are; the problem is they're writing the laws.

Nicholas Johnson,
Federal Communications Commissioner, 1972

Microsoft does not have monopoly power in the business of developing and licensing computer operating systems.

Bill Gates, chairman and CEO
Microsoft corporation, 1998

The Problem

Conventional market theory distinguishes between competitive market structures and numerous imperfectly competitive alternatives (monopolistic competition, oligopoly, and monopoly). Moreover, conventional theory demonstrates that society reaps greater benefits under pure competition: Maximum output is assured, prices are lower, and excessive profit making is avoided with all firms reacting to the dictates of a free market as "price takers." Under imperfectly competitive conditions, firms are able to exercise some degree of "price making," controlling prices and output for their own profitable advantage. In a textbook situation, there is little disagreement among economists about such generalizations. The trouble develops when we move from textbook examples to the real world.

A seemingly paradoxical situation appears when we examine the existing structure and organization of American business enterprise. On the one hand, the official ideology of American capitalism espouses a competitive ideal of many smallish producers, no one of which can materially affect price or output. On the other hand, everyday experience tells us that most markets are dominated by a comparative handful of very large firms. Exactly how much "bigness" might alter or eliminate desired competitive conditions has long been a concern in American capitalism. Since the passage of the Sherman Antitrust Act in 1890, a considerable body of law has been enacted "to protect competition." The essence of these accumulated laws may be summarized as follows.

1. It is illegal to enter into a contract, combination, or conspiracy in restraint of trade or to monopolize, attempt to monopolize, or combine or conspire to monopolize trade.
2. When the effect is to lessen competition or create a monopoly, it is illegal to acquire the stock or assets of competing companies, to discriminate among purchasers other than what can be justified by actual costs, or to enter into exclusive or tying contracts.
3. Under all cases, whether the effect is to monopolize or not, it is illegal to serve in the directorships of competing corporations, to use unfair methods of competition, or to employ unfair or deceptive acts or practices.

Despite the thrust of law and prevailing economic theory, the tendency toward larger and larger market structures has persisted since the closing decades of the nineteenth century. Although bigness has sometimes been occasioned by a firm's own individual production and sales efforts, by far the most popular route to increasing corporate size is through merger and combination. The earliest merger efforts of the late nineteenth century were largely *horizontal mergers*, which combined side-by-side competitors in the same industry. Very shortly, there followed *vertical mergers*, combining suppliers and purchasers of goods involved in the same chain of production. United States Steel, General Motors, and the American Tobacco Company came into existence following the former path. National Biscuit Company and Standard Oil (which also used horizontal combination) grew in size and influence using the latter strategy.

Three eras of horizontal and vertical mergers are easily identifiable: the 1890s, the 1920s, and the period immediately following World War II. Until comparatively recently, horizontal and vertical merger activity had slowed, in part because the really "juicy" combinations had already taken place and in part because antitrust law impeded greater concentration and growth of market power by existing giants. Merging, however, did not cease. Beginning in the 1960s and continuing to the present, firms have increasingly undertaken *conglomerate mergers*, uniting enterprises where no horizontal or vertical market advantages are present.

In recent years, the annual estimated value of mergers and acquisitions has increased from about $44 billion in 1980 to over $950 billion in 1997. Despite this tremendous rise, not all consolidations have resulted in either increased market share or profitability. Large industrial conglomerates such as General Electric and General Motors earn a growing share of their profits from financial and other non-manufacturing operations. Other corporations like AT&T and ITT have been forced to downsize or sell off divisions they acquired but on which they could not generate an acceptable rate of return. That noted, however, we cannot fail to recognize that in the last couple of years there have been some truly gargantuan mergers. BP-Amoco, Travelers-Citicorp, Albertson-American Stores, a spate of mergers among "the baby

Bells," the Conrail absorption by Norfolk Southern and CSX rail-ways, Chrysler-Daimler-Benz, and important combinations in the defense, information, and entertainment industries clearly indi-cate that we are in the middle of a new and important period of corporate combination.

Since the election of Ronald Reagan, government policy to-ward big business has focused on promoting competition through the deregulation of industries and markets, especially where there are only a few competitors perhaps none. Market forces, rather than government-initiated policies and anti-trust litigation, have been viewed as the quickest and most efficient means for ensuring adequate price competition and consumer sovereignty. These policies have led to a significant curtailment of prosecutions by the Justice Department for price fixing, price discrimination, and other antitrust violations. Whether or not such policy might undergo change is a matter of debate. However, the Clinton administration's antitrust action against Microsoft certainly suggests that a more energetic public policy could be emerging.

What is the significance of growing business concentration? To what extent are large firms able to act as price makers, setting excessive prices, restricting output, and creating market ineffi-ciency? To what degree do antitrust law, foreign competition, and other economic developments offset or negate the trend toward bigness?

While no economist, regardless of ideological preference, de-nies the existence of big business, there is widespread disagree-ment as to whether modern corporate size and increased merger activity represent a serious monopoly threat to the eco-nomic and social organization of American society.

Synopsis

Tho Conservative argument asserts that there are sufficient market and legal checks to make certain that big business does not act in an exploitative way but actually improves our economic well-being. Liberals accept the fact of bigness but maintain that government intervention is essential to control potential monopoly exploitation. The Radical argument holds that monopoly is the logical historical development of capitalism and that there is no way to halt this tendency without abolishing the production-for-profit system.

Anticipating the Arguments

- How do Conservatives argue that bigness in business is not proof of growing monopolistic power?
- What role do Liberals propose for government in dealing with the rise of giant enterprises, and how does their view differ from the Conservative approach?
- How do Radicals support their claim that the growth of alleged monopolistic business behavior in the United States is merely the logical progression of capitalist development?

THE CONSERVATIVE ARGUMENT

American public policy toward big business tends to be cyclical, in some periods reflecting a strong antibusiness bias (the early 1900s and the 1930s, for instance) and, in others, tending to be more tolerant of large-scale enterprise. During the last couple of decades, with a few exceptions, public policy makers have shown reasonable restraint in their antitrust pursuits. The result has been beneficial to both American business and the American public. But, as the Microsoft case of 1997–98 has shown, the unreasoned fear of bigness in business can reassert itself anytime. Accordingly, it is well to remember why such fears can lead to dangerous economic policy making.

In general, fear of bigness rests on gross misunderstandings of the structure and performance of American business. Foremost among these is the confusion of bigness with monopoly, and the resulting corollary that big is bad. The anti-big-business attitude that emerges from these views is always a serious threat to the American economic system. Far from leading to the rebirth of a competitive business society, most antimonopoly efforts erode free enterprise itself. Ironically, an attack on big business boils down to an attack on business of all kinds. More than they realize, the owners of mom-and-pop grocery stores and the like arc themselves threatened by assaults on business giants.

Bigness Does Not Equal Monopoly

Bigness in and of itself is not proof of monopoly power. Of course, there is no denying the existence of "dominant firms" in certain American industries and of the concentration of market share and capital in the hands of a few firms in others. However, a variety of *real world* market forces come into play which negate or significantly diminish the "price making" powers that economic theory suggests these business giants might possess. The point here is to get beyond "monopoly theory" and look at the world as it is. For instance, there are many cases of interindustry competition among different "concentrated" industries. Glass, aluminum, steel, paper, and plastic producers, for example, all battle each other for the food-container market. Nor should international competition be forgotten. While tariffs and shipping costs may offer some protection to American firms, the protection is not absolute—witness the 20 percent share of the auto market seized by foreign car makers. The point is simple: Big business, far from ending competition, has heightened it. The solitary village blacksmith, barrel maker, or flour miller of a century ago had far greater monopoly power over price, quality, and output than does his present-day big business counterpart.

Those who worry about excessive monopoly power should consider one further point. In a market society, the great check against price gouging, by IBM or by a barrel maker, is consumer demand. If prices go too high, sellers simply cannot sell their products—or enough of them to make a profit—and prices will come down.

If we can get beyond the silly but appealing logic of the "big is bad" argument, we might truly understand that the opposite is much more nearly correct: Big business has been good for America.

In Defense of Bigness

The primary reason for merger and combination among enterprises in the past has been to obtain technical economies that lower production costs. To be sure, there have been examples of firms attempting to exploit their market power as monopolistic price makers; however, such mergers are rare indeed, and when detected (as they easily are), antitrust and civil law provide ample protections to society at large. In the meantime, *big* business has been the major vehicle for economic and technical advance in the United States. Few can deny that product progress and relatively falling prices for most consumer and producer goods during the twentieth century have been the result of expensive technological advancements; these could only have resulted from the great capital concentration and large-scale marketing strategies of big enterprise.

Recently, Liberal and Radical critics of business enterprise have directed their wrath against the newer conglomerate mergers. Such attacks are also threats to business growth, since conglomerate mergers presently account for about three-quarters of all combinations. This strategy is an extension of the "big is bad" argument; however, it fails to consider that conglomerate mergers may also provide consumer benefits. By strengthening inefficient and costly businesses through improved management techniques and by providing badly needed capital, prices will be lowered. Moreover, the conglomerate merger often increases competition by resuscitating firms that otherwise would fail. And strong firms are strengthened by acquiring many diverse operations that permit the firm to avoid "putting all its eggs in one basket." In this era of immense and swift technological and product change, diversification is an important insurance policy for a large enterprise.

The size and scale of the truly large American firms become a bit less threatening if two factors are considered: (1) the threat posed by giant foreign manufacturing enterprises and (2) the health and abundance of small enterprises in the United States.

A policy aimed at weakening large firms simply because they are large will not protect the American consumer—and certainly not the American worker. A host of foreign giants stands ready to flood American markets with goods should large American firms fail to maintain their vitality and profitability. Indeed, the relative slippage of American producers in world competition is an important argument on behalf of reducing constraints on the size of American business.

In any case, bigness is vastly overemphasized. Of America's 12 million businesses, 11.8 million qualify as small businesses according to the Small Business Administration. Regardless of the size of the giant enterprises, no other economy can boast this proportion of small, independent enterprises to the entire population. Small business employs almost 70 percent of the total work force. The smallest of the small, those employing twenty or fewer workers, the fastest-growing segment of the business economy, hire three out of every four current entrants into the labor market. Given these characteristics of American business enterprise, it becomes obvious that big business, even if it were a problem, gets undue attention from Liberals and Radicals. Smallness and competition remain the dominant characteristics of American enterprise.

Singling out big business is unfair and misleading. Even if business bigness were demonstrably bad, why isn't the same logic applied to big government or big labor unions? Those who cry "monopoly" in the business sector rarely apply that argument against the United Auto Workers or the Teamsters, nor do they see the bureaucratic state management of pricing—from hospital rooms to agricultural products—as analogous to the imagined monopoly power of big enterprise.

The Promise of a New Approach by Government

The record of government enforcement of antitrust law has, since the beginning of the century, been inconsistent and contradictory, tending always to reflect the political ideology of the current occupant of the White House. Naturally enough, the intensity of antitrust action heightens with Liberal occupancy. However, even under Conservative administrations, there remained a troublesome ambivalence about how to deal with giant enterprises. Frequently actions were initiated by both Conservative and Liberal administrations against firms purely on the grounds that they were big or that they were too profitable. Such an approach works against the development of dynamic and thriving firms. It is rather like punishing the winning runner in a race because she ran too fast. The profitable business is not the only loser, however; so is the society that has benefited in jobs and lower product prices from the large firm's efficiency. However, two landmark antitrust cases of the 1980s restored some reason to our public policy toward big business.

In the 1982 dismissal of a government action against IBM for monopolizing the mainframe computer industry, the Justice Department agreed that despite IBM's size and its share of the market, there was no proof that the firm had acted monopolistically. The decision should stand as an important legal landmark against those who would penalize a firm thoughtlessly simply because it has been successful. In the AT&T case, decided at the same time as the IBM case, the Justice Department affirmed the doctrine of competition. AT&T's monopoly power in the buying and selling of communications equipment and services was ended. AT&T was proved guilty of using its power (provided by government as a regulated monopoly) to exclude competitors from the data and electronic transmission market. AT&T was compelled to divest itself of its purely "public utility" local phone operations and join battle fairly with competing firms in the long-distance and information systems markets. For the foreseeable future, a useful antitrust policy is in place: *Bigness itself does not prove collusion or unfair price setting, but when such activities are proved, they will be halted.*

Paralleling and complementing the IBM and AT&T cases has been a relaxation at the Justice Department of vigorous opposition to large corporate mergers. This, of course, has sparked criticism from some Liberal critics who fail to see the advantages obtained from most of these mergers. Far from being a submission to business pressure, the more passive approach toward mergers and "bigness" in its many forms is a recognition of the economic gains from size that provide important benefits to the entire society, not the least of which is an improvement of American firms' ability to compete with foreign giants. However, Conservatives are not unmindful that bigness *can* lead to abuses.

Conservatives do not deny the existence of monopoly abuse when it is real. Very clearly, the exercise of monopoly power is unjustifiable and injurious to individuals. It prevents efficient allocation of resources. However, aside from those cases of monopoly initiated or encouraged by the government and occasional conspiratorial endeavors by individual enterprises, the "monopoly problem" is mostly a phony issue. Liberals use it as a pretext for urging massive social or governmental interference with the market, while Radicals find it convenient as an excuse for their revolutionary assault on the entire system. Both groups would use the issue in a self-serving fashion to extinguish individualism and private property rights.

THE LIBERAL ARGUMENT

Traditional economic analysis since Adam Smith has argued that the "great regulator" for business activity is the market. Here, small, competitive firms struggle against each other to sell goods and gain customers. Prices and the possibility of exploitation are always regulated by the "invisible hand" of supply and demand. Although we may nit-pick over whether this type of pure competition ever existed outside of economists' minds, it certainly does not exist in the United States today. Just 2,000 businesses in all areas of the economy produce about half of our GDP; the "invisible hand" has largely been replaced by the highly visible fist of corporate power.

The Problem of Policy Selection

While most modern-day Conservatives equivocate on the issue of big business, preferring not to see any monopoly problems except in the rarest of cases, Liberals face the problem directly. *Business concentration does exist in the United States.* The scale and intensity of efforts to increase concentration through merger is growing. Nor are all merger efforts benign conglomerate combinations. The policy issue, then, is not a matter of recognizing the obvious but of determining how to deal with it.

The most rudimentary analysis of monopoly behavior tells us that, all things being equal, monopolistic firms tend to charge higher prices and produce less than might otherwise be expected under competitive conditions. They employ fewer workers at lower wages and generally foster resource misallocation. Moreover, the greater the degree of monopoly power, the greater the consumer exploitation.

The implications of this line of economic analysis are clear. The return of competition is apparently the only way to return to economic virtue. In a policy sense, this might mean the enforcement of a vigorous anti-monopoly policy, leading to the restructuring of some industries into greater numbers of similar-sized units of production. Liberals are not in total agreement on this point, but most would oppose a grand breaking up of giant enterprises. First of all, the practical application of a literal "break them up" policy is not politically or legally feasible. We long ago passed the point of being able to return to some romantic eighteenth-century concept of the marketplace. This is not to say that stimulation of competition in certain industries might not be desirable or possible through the application of antitrust laws. In fact, the Justice Department must always be prepared to initiate antimonopoly legal action, but this could not be carried out on a broad scale without weakening our legal and economic structures. Second, there is no solid evidence that pure competition, enforced indiscriminately, would be beneficial, even if it could be attained without seriously wrenching society.

What these observations mean in a practical context is that Liberals approach the question of "bigness in American business" quite prag-

Table 4.1

Corporations with $250 Million or More of Assets in 1994

	Number	Total assets (billions of dollars)	Percent of industry's firms	Percent of industry's assets
Agriculture, forestry, and fishing	17	8,472	0.01	10.60
Mining	112	185,544	0.32	77.40
Construction	39	42,121	<0.001	16.91
Manufacturing	1,256	3,845,722	0.40	84.98
Transportation and public utilities	415	1,668,010	0.22	91.33
Wholesale and retail trade	507	996,429	0.05	55.51
Finance, insurance, and real estate	4,403	12,295,945	0.65	88.49
Services	294	424,370	0.02	50.89
Totals	7,043	19,466,613	0.16	83.03

Source: Statistical Abstract of the United States, 1997, Table 843, p. 543.

matically. As Table 4.1 indicates, the degree of concentration varies from industry to industry, and concentration alone does not tell the whole story about abuses of market power. Accordingly, concentration in the oil industry might be approached differently from concentration in the auto industry. Domestic automobile production is effectively limited to just three firms, with General Motors producing about 50 percent of American output. Some years ago, GM's size and share were so large that, in the minds of many Americans, the firm appeared to be a logical candidate for "break them up" antitrust action, a situation not unlike the one in which Microsoft presently finds itself in the personal computer industry. Charges that GM has worked effectively in the past as a price leader are difficult to question. However, that was a long time ago, when GM effectively controlled 70 to 75 percent of the American car and truck market. In any case, even if this sales practice still existed as an option for GM, price leadership would not necessarily mean consumer exploitation. Nor would breaking up GM necessarily lead to social improvement. Even though GM's size has probably pushed it well beyond what is necessary for attaining efficiency from economies of scale, there is no assurance that forty or even a dozen smaller GMs could produce a product of similar price and quality and hire the work force that the present firm does. And, at any rate, the once-dominant position of GM has been severely eroded by the extensive penetration of the American auto market by foreign car makers. In this case at least, most Liberals will agree with Conservatives that concern over national concentration ratios and domestic firm size must be weighed against the realities of world competition. On the other hand, the oil industry, with less actual concentration than the auto industry, conspired during the 1970s energy crises to force up the prices of gasoline and natural gas by withholding supplies.

The point is that there are different types of giant enterprises, some highly predatory and exploitative and others reasonably responsible to the public interest. Concentration alone is no justification for applying a vigorous antitrust action against members of the American auto industry. But the behavior of the oil industry in the 1970s is the worst kind of monopolistic activity. There are no easy "monopoly tests." Each case must be taken on its own merits.

Having rejected the rigid competitive argument, we are left to accept the reality of modern corporate concentration. However, though Liberals realize that bigness itself need not be proof of monopoly abuse, they do not subscribe to the policy advanced by Conservatives. The quest for greater market power is not always enlightened; it may, in fact, destroy business itself, as large firms act consciously or unconsciously to protect and expand their influence. Certainly, the current preoccupation of American business with "merger mania" has had a negative effect because it diverts funds into takeovers rather than capital investment and it absorbs the brightest business minds in short-run profit objectives rather than long-run production planning. Meanwhile, unrestrained business power may lead to the domination of government by narrow business interests and the subversion of the rights of the many for the benefit of a few. Thus Liberals believe the creation of a clear public policy toward mergers and bigness in business is essential to protect the balance of pluralistic interests in an open society. An equitable balance of labor, consumer, and capital interests must be the philosophical cornerstone of any intelligent policy toward business.

Through fair and calculated government intervention, big businesses can be made compatible with the social objectives of economic order, reasonable prices and high quality, and technological advancement. Government actions, depending on the situation, must go beyond mere antitrust enforcement. They may take the form of selective tax and subsidy arrangements, under certain circumstances exercising direct controls over pricing, hiring, and capital investment policies, and sometimes exerting some degree of intervention in the international operations of business. Monopoly policy, moreover, must not be separated from general public policy objectives directed at inflation control, maintaining full employment, and encouraging economic growth. Some people will argue that this external imposition of social objectives on the private sector is pure socialism, but they miss the point.

Social Control Is Not Socialism

Pragmatic social control of big business is not the same as social ownership. Corporate ownership today is widely dispersed and far removed from the day-to-day management decisions of American business. Excessive concern over *who* owns the productive property only clouds the important business and public issues at stake. *How* the privately owned property is performing is the really important question. Even though privately owned, most large businesses are already "social institutions" with "social responsibilities." To put the point simply, GM does not have the right to fail any more than it has the right to conspire against the public. To demand social responsibility is perfectly consistent with the real-world structure of business and the economy, and it does not challenge private ownership in any serious way.

Businesses, moreover, are more responsive in the area of social responsibility than is generally understood. Social concern on their part is not purely altruism but good business. Flagrant monopolistic behavior invites government scrutiny and public outrage. The old era of "the public be damned" is past. Few firms, whatever their size and market power, want long and costly antitrust litigation. Even consumer boycotts and public pressure for legislative intervention are sizable threats and induce thoughtful constraint. Moreover, there is significant pressure within the business community to police itself. Abuse of economic power disrupts markets and creates economic instability; this situation, while perhaps favorable to one or a few firms, interferes with general business activity. Social responsibility, finally, is not an ethical question but a matter of profit and loss.

These points should not be misunderstood. The Liberal fully understands that big business may indeed be a threat—in its pricing, labor, international, and other policies. But big business does not *have* to be a threat to the economic system. It can be brought under social control.

Public policy toward big business, then, remains a matter of directing private enterprise toward social objectives that include reasonable prices, efficiency, high employment, and adequate profit return while also taking into consideration such broad concerns as ecology, resource conservation, and the overall performance of the economy. The creation of such a policy must be the responsibility of an enlightened federal government. Government must act as an unbiased umpire, attempting always to balance the diverse economic and social interests of the nation. Such intervention need not abridge basic property rights (which is what Radicals want). But it would set social priorities above the pursuit of selfish individualistic goals (so feverishly defended by Conservatives).

THE RADICAL ARGUMENT

One of the great evasions of economic theory is its idealized portrayal of competition as a process devoid of conflict, power, and politics. Indeed, the existence of *any* market power is defined strictly in technical terms: If market prices are observed to be above marginal cost, then actual competition is falling short of its standard of perfect competition. Microeconomic theory aside, it is well understood by citizens and CEOs alike that the tendency for businesses to become both more centralized in control and concentrated in sales and assets is, and has been, a persistent outcome of capitalist competition. Today, large corporations dominate most markets, and it is through their control of economic resources that they can command such a disproportionate and deleterious impact on American society. While both Conservatives and Liberals oppose monopoly power, neither group wants to recognize that political power has become concentrated in a relatively small capitalist class who now seek to dominate the political process through their unchallenged economic power.

All mainstream economic theory is loath to recognize not only that firms seek to grow, but that the objective is to *dominate* both a particular industry and the economy and greater society as well. To achieve these goals, it is crucial that a firm have the strength to impose its own price on the market in order to increase its profits. To do this, a business must have the capacity and power to price-gouge as well as sustain a ruinous price war. Competition cannot be managed, democratized, or negotiated—corporations are fundamentally authoritarian organizations driven by the imperatives of growth and profitability. Thus, the Radical position can be easily distinguished by its understanding of a relatively simple business strategy that *all* capitalist firms must obey: Grow or die. Unpalatable as it may be, small firms do not play a major role in the U.S. economy and also tend not to persist. Either they evolve into large units of production and distribution (whatever the product) or they are eliminated. In the final analysis, if the state truly wants to tame and manage big business, it has to change the terms and conditions under which large firms exist and operate.

Monopoly Capitalism: What Went Wrong?

Prior to the late 1970s, most economists—including many Radicals—believed that capitalism had entered a new stage where the cutthroat, predatory price competition that characterized the nineteenth-century economy would no longer be appropriate for large modern corporations. The new post–World War II era of "monopoly capitalism" was one where profitability would be ensured by collusive or monopoly pricing arrangements. Because there was little micro or macro evidence of persistent price declines, economists of all stripes had come to believe that firms no longer competed on the basis of price. Furthermore, though economists were loath to acknowledge it, an uneasy but workable arrangement between management and workers prevailed: labor would subordinate its demands for higher wages and benefits, if capital allowed living standards to rise. Indeed, post-inflation income generally rose from about 1950 to 1973, largely due to labor's ability to impose its demands upon capital through unions and political organizing. However, by the early 1970s most of these gains were reversed. The average real wage peaked in 1973 at about $14.00 per hour and has failed to recover to that level after nearly 25 years. Workers in capital-intensive manufacturing industries were especially hard hit as capitalists shifted production overseas or invested in more profitable, non-industrial sectors. By the 1990s, so-called professional "white collar" occupations that were thought immune to economic adversity were now facing layoffs, downsizing, and widespread job insecurity. What went wrong? Why couldn't monopoly capital maintain its pricing power and guarantee high levels of production and employment?

For one thing, by the early 1980s the political consensus that had held the economy together was over. Deregulation and globalization created a "dog eat dog" economy with rampant job insecurity and declining living standards for the vast majority of wage earners. These reactionary policies were actually initiated by Democratic president Jimmy Carter but were fully unleashed under the Reagan administration. While workers bore the brunt of these reactionary policies, there was a battle being fought within the capitalist class. First, industrial capitalists who had become complacent with their dominant market positions were quickly supplanted by more nimble and efficient foreign competitors. This was partly the result of years of underinvestment and managerial incompetence and arrogance, but also reflected the end of unchallenged military and economic dominance by the United States.

A second problem faced by capitalists was how to tame the unprecedented inflation that gripped the U.S. economy from about 1968 through the mid-1980s. Financial capital sought to reestablish profitability in their industries by breaking the back of persistent price increases and inflationary expectations. Once again, Jimmy Carter—a "liberal" Democratic president—rescued financial capital by appointing a conservative banker, Paul Volcker, to head the Federal Reserve Board. Volcker's high-interest-rate policies, combined with rampant deregulation of financial markets, brought about a decisive victory for the financial sector. "Smokestack" industries such as autos, steel, and heavy manufacturing could not survive the simultaneous onslaught of a stagnating economy, widespread inflation, foreign competition, and disaccumulation. The subsequent period of deindustrialization and disinflation that destroyed the industrial heartland set the stage for what has turned out to be the greatest increase in the value of paper assets in U.S. history.

Persistent Concentration, Persistent Competition

If firms have little choice but to grow or die, it should come as no surprise that success in the marketplace necessarily entails having a large scale of production and sizable market share. Growth, however, can be achieved in any number of ways, such as by increasing sales or by gobbling up a competitor. Since 1990, businesses have spent an astounding $3 trillion either to merge with or to acquire another firm. While capitalists and their apologists claim that combinations serve to "cleanse" the system of inefficient producers, in actuality much of this money will be used to transfer ownership from one capitalist to another. For workers, mergers and acquisitions typically result in plant closings and layoffs rather than generating new investment in factories and technologies. Capitalists like Al "Chainsaw" Dunlap are revered and rewarded by Wall Street for acquiring companies, only to sell off assets and fire workers. More often than not, the stock price of the "right-sized" company rises. In recent years, deregulation and global competition have undermined the largest firms' traditional strategies of price fixing and production limits in their efforts to ensure profitability. Nevertheless, large multinational corporations now seek to acquire both resources and their competitors in order to better withstand the increasingly dynamic and turbulent competitive environment. Earning high rates of return has become dependent on access to large pools of financial, technological, and human resources.

To gain some perspective on the degree of centralization in the American economy, let us examine Table 4.1, which shows the proportion of firms in the major sectors of the American economy with assets of at least $250 million (based on corporate federal income tax returns). Combining agriculture and construction (which account for less than 2 percent of total assets), it is clear that the distribution of assets is profoundly unequal across sectors. Less than 1 percent of the firms in mining; manufacturing; transportation and public utilities; and finance, insurance, and real estate own over 75 percent of each industry's respective total assets. In the sectors that employ the greatest number of workers—wholesale/retail trade and services—about half of total assets are controlled by less than 0.05 percent of all firms. Overall, less than 0.20 percent of all firms control over 80 percent of total corporate assets.

As mergers and acquisitions continue, and concentration of sales and assets in many industries increases, large corporations will attempt to reassert their power in the market by using a variety of strategy and tactics. Rather than being a new era of manageable capitalism, we have returned to the nineteenth century where unbridled competition wreaks havoc on anyone who works for a living. Reducing the labor content in each unit of output is the dominant objective in the internationalization of production. For example, multinational clothing manufacturers and retailers are able to achieve incredible profits by paying their overseas workers 50 cents per hour while simultaneously charging so-called "competitive prices"—between $20.00 and $100.00—for a pair of jeans or sneakers sold in the U.S. market. Meanwhile, the overseas workers toil under oppressive working conditions that would be illegal under U.S. labor law. Nike, the Gap, and Disney have become unconscionably profitable by producing and pricing their products in this manner.

Domestic service industries are also trying to significantly reduce wage costs while seeking to grow through the development, acquisition, and consolidation of integrated delivery networks. Because it is more difficult to use foreign cheap labor in the production of services (e.g., a haircut or a heart transplant), capitalists employ a different but equally effective strategy. Initially, the goal is to quickly gain market share by offering a service well below the actual cost of production. Low prices, in turn generate significant volume growth as the customer base rapidly expands. Managed-health-care companies, airlines, cable television, and on-line computer service providers have been singularly successful in pursuing this type of strategy. Once market dominance is achieved in a region, prices can be increased with little retaliation from either competitors or the government. In fact, all of these industries are subject to some form of regulatory oversight, yet there is little political will to control predatory market conduct for fear of losing valuable campaign contributions from corporate donors. What's more, the Justice Department has shown little interest in prosecuting corporations for unfair pricing policies. The relatively low inflation rates of the 1990s have also helped to shield large corporations from scrutiny of their pricing power. Nevertheless, it is quite evident that competition both within and between industries will intensify, which surely will lead to lower wages and benefits while capital acts to consolidate its position and seek to create conditions where it can continue to dominate the American economy.

Big Capital and Politics: Change the Rules

As concentration and centralization grows and industries invade each other's territory, corporations will not only use the political system to repress worker demands, but, more importantly, will use legal and governmental authority to gain competitive advantages. Historically, big business has always maintained legions of lobbying organizations to press their demands before legislators. While it is difficult for big business to win at the ballot box, it has had little problem in getting politicians to create fiscal and regulatory policies that are favorable to its interests. The rash of scandals related to campaign finance irregularities involved many large corporations seeking preferential treatment and/or governmental contracts. Moreover, the $350 billion settlement with the tobacco industry and the $100 million penalty paid by Archer Daniels Midland indicate the scale and depth of capital's resources to withstand any pressure from the state. Campaign contributions continue to be an extremely cost-effective method for businesses to obtain favors, preferential tax treatments, contracts, and a host of other benefits from the government. As voters become increasingly dissatisfied with the political process, corporations will wield greater power over federal and state legislatures.

The solution to the seemingly unstoppable power of big business does not lie within the framework of conventional economic analysis and policy. While worker control over investment, production, and employment is the only long-term solution to rein in big business, in the short run more specific measures are required. In particular, what is needed is a strategy to undercut corporate power by changing the legal status of corporations so they lose their privileges of unlimited longevity, due process, and limited liability granted to them under federal and state laws. Historically, courts have ruled that corporations are "individuals," entitled to all the rights and protections guaranteed under the U.S. Constitution. Following the Reconstruction Era (1865–70), corporations shrewdly used the due process clause of the Fourteenth Amendment (ratified by the states in 1868) to overturn limitations placed upon them by state governments. Rulings by state regulatory agencies and legislatures were continually overturned by the federal courts, which in effect defended the rapacity of nineteenth century Robber Barons by arguing that state controls deprived a corporation of property without due process. While some states fought to limit corporate power, other states (such as Delaware) actively courted corporations by exempting them from taxes and granting them perpetual charters.

Limiting longevity and the ability to transfer risk will significantly curtail the capacity of a corporation to grow and achieve market dominance. Corporate managers will be very wary of undertaking illegal actions since their liabilities will not be limited to their equity holdings. While Marx forcefully argued that capital would never accede anything to labor without a fight, he also recognized that capitalism depends upon specific juridical and legal institutions, especially property rights. Changing the legal status of a corporation would be a strategy both bold and politically practical, with a realistic chance of limiting the power of big capital. However, changing the status of corporations will not be sufficient to change the economic and social relations between labor and capital. As competition further winnows the ever-shrinking number of large firms, and democracy withers under the oppression of a tiny number of megacorporations, it will become evident to all citizens that social control and ownership of the economy's asset base is the only viable solution. Planning by and for the needs of all citizens—not corporate planning—will become central to ensuring and fulfilling the political economic ideals of American society.

Economic Regulation

Has Deregulation Worked?

The committee has found among the leading representatives of the railroad interests an increasing readiness to accept the aid of Congress in working out the solution of the railroad problem which has obstinately baffled all their efforts, and not a few of the ablest railroad men of the country seem disposed to look to the intervention of Congress as promising to afford the best means of ultimately securing a more equitable and satisfactory adjustment of the relations of the transportation interests to the community than they themselves have been able to bring about.

U.S. Senate Select Committee on Interstate Commerce, 1886

Railroads were totally regulated for almost a century. Obviously it will take time for railroads to learn all of the things that can be done in a freer climate. It will also take shippers time to learn this as well. But already it is apparent that both can use deregulation to their respective advantages.

Association of American Railroads, 1982

The headlong descent into ideological and haphazard deregulation is over as far as Congress is concerned.

Congressman Charles E. Schumer, 1987

No reasonable person will lament the passing of the Interstate Commerce Commission.

George Will, ABC News Commentator, 1996

The Problem

The objective of antitrust law and its enforcement, as discussed in Issue 4, is to maintain an acceptable degree of competition in most markets. A second type of government intervention in the structure and performance of markets rests on the assumption that certain markets perform best under less-than-competitive conditions that are strictly regulated by government agencies. In these regulated industries, a kind of "monopoly bargain" is struck whereby one firm, or at most a few, is granted various protections from competition in return for surrendering to a regulatory agency power over pricing, output, and other production, financing, and marketing decisions.

The most common example of a regulated industry and a regulatory agency is a regional public utility (a gas and electric company or a regional phone company), which is regulated by a state "public service commission." However, the concept of public regulation has been applied much more broadly than in the so-called public utility sector. The first federal venture into direct regulation came with the Interstate Commerce Commission (ICC) in 1887 (a full three years before federal antitrust law was laid down in the Sherman Act). The ICC was charged with restoring order to the nation's ailing railroads, an industry long characterized on the one hand by periodic episodes of financial collapse resulting from vicious rate wars and on the other by the very worst type of monopolistic practices. Over the next century, more than a dozen independent federal agencies and commissions were erected to bring a measure of government regulation to everything from banking to the airwaves to nuclear power.

Initially, the logic of insulating certain industries from the forces of the market rested on two economic considerations: (1) that there existed the economic advantages of lower costs (*economies of scale*) resulting from a single producer or a limited number of producers and (2) that a discernible *public interest* would be served by exempting the industry from competition and by establishing government regulation of price, service, and output. As the years passed, however, these two criteria were stretched, modified, and sometimes neglected altogether as the extent of government regulation expanded in many directions. The idea of "regulating private industry in the public interest" was a peculiarly American experiment. Elsewhere in the world state ownership has been the preferred technique for dealing with public interest questions. In the course of European economic development, postal services, railways, telecommunications, and electric and gas utilities were generally state-owned. In the United States, the postal service is the only industry ever entirely owned and operated "in the public interest."

For most of the past century, industrial regulation enjoyed a high degree of public support, with most practicing economists nodding their approval at the work of regulatory agencies. The regulatory high-water mark was reached in the early 1970s. However, in the economy of the late 1970s, troubled by inflation, recession, unemployment, energy crises, and growing federal budgetary problems, regulatory activity was placed under greater scrutiny. What a closer examination showed pretty much reflected what one wanted to see. Most Liberals, who had long been supporters of the regulation "in the public interest" philosophy, defended the practice. Conservatives, sensing the direction of a new ideological wind that was blowing up, were quick to attack federal regulation of industry. Never strong supporters of regulatory efforts anyway, most Conservatives felt that the regulatory link was among the weakest in the chain of Liberal interventionism in the economy. Their attack was direct enough: Regulation produces greater costs to society through creating and maintaining market inefficiency than any benefits it might provide for the public interest. By the mid-1970s, a new buzzword had entered academic and political discussions of the regulatory process: *deregulation.*

Between 1978 and 1985, the deregulators (which now included a fair number of Liberals as well as most Conservatives) had succeeded in eliminating most regulation of airlines, buses, trucking, radio broadcasting, and natural gas production and distribution. Considerable relaxation occurred in the regulation of railroads, television and cable broadcasting, and banking and financial services. Meanwhile, the splitting up of the Bell Telephone System in 1984 as the result of federal antitrust action opened much of the previously highly regulated phone system to market competition. The deregulatory mood spread during the

Reagan years to a variety of government agencies charged with overseeing broad areas of social regulation, such as the Department of Consumer Affairs and the Federal Trade Commission.

By the late 1980s, however, the deregulation movement seemed to be running out of steam. The financial shock of a 500-point decline in the stock market on October 19, 1987, brought forth calls for greater regulation of the securities market by the federal government. This shock was followed quickly by a monumental solvency crisis in the savings and loan industry that seemed to be the direct outcome of "excessive deregulation" of banking institutions. In the airlines industry, formerly hailed by antiregulation advocates as the model for successful deregulation, the initial consumer benefits of increased competition and lower fares seemed to be ebbing in favor of greater monopoly power and higher prices. At the same time, deregulation of the television industry seemed to be pointing toward a decline of over-the-airwaves television and the potential loss of a long-held American "right," that of free television programming. Such developments began to generate second thoughts about deregulation.

Yet, if there were serious second thoughts about deregulation, they did not produce a marked redirection of public policy. In 1996, the old Interstate Commerce Commission (ICC) the granddaddy of all federal regulatory efforts—was legislated out of existence. And, in the fall of 1996, President Clinton won reelection while agreeing with his Republican opponent that "the era of Big Government is over." On the other hand, the popular enthusiasm of a decade earlier for pulling back government from its many regulatory activities was notably diminished. Opinion polls were beginning to show that Americans, although not yet seeking a 180-degree turn in government policy toward "reregulation," still preferred a comparatively high order of regulatory intervention. Weariness with "big government" had not translated into no government regulation at all.

Synopsis

Conservatives argue that regulation is counterproductive, producing more costs than benefits to both the regulated industries and the public. Accordingly, they support the drift to deregulation and advocate more deregulation. The Liberal argument defends the general performance record of most regulated industries and maintains that many recent experiments in deregulation are dangerous to the economy. Radicals see the historical development of regulation as essentially a prop to monopoly privilege and recent deregulation efforts as merely a smokescreen for doing away with what business now considers the less attractive aspects of serving the public interest.

Anticipating the Arguments

- What are some of the counterproductive results of regulation that Conservatives see, and how would their plan for deregulation end such problems?
- On what grounds do Liberals defend at least limited regulation over complete deregulation?
- Why do Radicals reject regulation and instead call for public ownership and operation of previously regulated industries?

THE CONSERVATIVE ARGUMENT

The Conservative position on regulation is based on two sturdy and now-familiar principles. First, regulation—or any interference with the market—tends to create resource misallocation, inefficiency, and, ultimately, greater costs to the community. Second, left alone, the market is capable of more rational decisions about the success or survival of a firm or industry than is the voting public or its representatives and bureaucrats.

The Failure of Regulation

Except for the very limited and infrequent situations where a "natural monopoly" exists, there are no justifiable conditions for regulating industry. A natural monopolist, such as a local power and lighting company, enjoys the advantages of large-scale production techniques that can provide all of a market's output at lower unit costs than could exist if there were a number of producers. In such a situation, the community can obtain the lower costs only if it restrains the monopolists' natural propensity to maximize profits by setting prices at

whatever the market will bear. The problem with the American application of this regulation principle, however, is that regulation has
mostly been applied in situations where some degree of competition
actually exists or where competition should be encouraged. The result
has been that the community gets a regulated monopoly or a tight
oligopoly when it would have been better served by creating and maintaining competitive conditions. Even the regulation of so-called natural
monopolics has had its problems because of inefficient rulings on pricing and service by the regulatory agency, usually in the name of protecting the "public interest."

To get to the point directly, let's examine our first effort at using an
independent regulatory agency to supervise an industry: the ICC. As the
oldest U.S. regulatory agency, the ICC has the longest list of "classic"
regulatory errors and is a good example of all the debilitating effects
age brings to commission activity. The original intent of the ICC was to
bring order to the chaotic and excessively competitive rate-making
practices of the railroads. Its goal was to protect the public from railroad
price collusion and to protect the railroads from one another. By the
mid-1930s, ICC power extended to all surface commercial transportation in the country. Specific ICC controls covered rate setting, mergers,
financial issues, abandonment, and service discontinuance, as well as
carrier layoffs of labor. There was virtually nothing that a rail carrier or
any other carrier regulated by the Interstate Commerce Commission
could do without first obtaining commission approval.

Before attempts at rail and trucking deregulation were introduced in
the 1970s, the ICC followed a narrow, two-sided strategy: first, to
maintain a "competitive balance" between and among the different
modes (trucks and railroads) of surface transportation that provided
each carrier with an adequate return on its investment, and second, to
provide service at a cost and to the extent broad public interest objectives were served.

In misguided efforts to "maintain competition among different
modes," the ICC long followed the strategy of "umbrella rate making,"
a practice of setting a rate high cnough to allow less efficient modes of
transport to earn a profit on specific services. This provided a special
handicap to railroads, which lost traffic to other modes simply because
they were not allowed to set lower rates (prices) and use their greater
efficiency in the movement of certain goods. In protecting trucks and
water carriers, the ICC directed business away from the more efficient

railroads. At the same time, shippers and consumers absorbed higher-than-necessary transport charges in their purchases.

Similar anticompetitive outcomes resulted from the ICC's opposition to rail mergers. This led to costly "balkanization." The line-haul railroads were unable to combine to increase freight exchange and coordination and to strengthen their financial structures. By denying the industry access to these economies of scale, service remained expensive and inefficient. The ICC also prohibited intermodal mergers. Railroads were not allowed to consolidate with trucks and other carriers to improve their overall efficiency.

Meanwhile, in search of the will-o'-the-wisp "public interest," the ICC also acted to raise transport costs and reduce rail efficiency by maintaining redundant routes and little-used spurs. Permission for abandonments of low-density or loss-producing operations was difficult to obtain from the commission, and railroads were compelled to pour millions of dollars into expensive routes that generated only a few dollars in traffic.

By prohibiting railroads from setting their rates freely, denying them the right to develop joint rail–truck transportation companies, and demanding that they continue to operate costly and inefficient services and schedules, the ICC rendered the railroads' competitive situation virtually hopeless. ICC decisions on rates, abandonments, and mergers were presented as proof of the agency's commitment to the public interest. In point of fact, its action harmed rather than protected the nation's welfare.

The general ICC strategy was applied by other regulatory agencies with not much better success. Whether we look at railroads, airlines, long-distance telecommunications, broadcasting, trucking, or banking, we see the same dismal results from the era of public regulation. First, regulation encouraged cartel pricing. This usually meant setting a price floor that was high enough to allow the least efficient member of the cartel to survive. The industry price was usually higher than the price that would have existed under competitive conditions. Second, in the absence of any effective price competition in the industry, competition could only emerge in nonprice areas. Banks emphasized "special services." Airlines promoted themselves as "friendlier" or as offering more sumptuous in-flight meals. Few regulated firms were likely to introduce new services that produced real benefits or savings to customers. New ways of doing business were always seen as posing elements of risk and instability that neither the regulated industry nor the regulators wanted. Meanwhile, new investment and modernization lagged in regulated industries. Third, industries in a regulated cartel developed a special inertia at the management level. In fact, as deregulation became an increasingly popular idea in the 1970s and 1980s, many of its strongest opponents were the very industries that were to be deregulated.

The Market Alternative

Efforts to introduce a market alternative to regulation have posed and will continue to pose special problems. Not only are government bureaucrats unwilling to destroy their own jobs, but a number of regulated firms and many of their customers have also shown some fear of living in a free marketplace. What, in fact, can unregulated markets do better than regulated ones?

The first advantage the consuming public enjoys is falling prices. Except in cases where certain consumers experienced benefits from price discrimination, competitive market prices will be lower than those established for regulated cartels. Airline passengers, for instance, have learned to enjoy these benefits on long-distance routes since the start of the 1980s, but, of course, some short-distance (and very high-cost) flights have gone up in price to reflect real rather than administered pricing conditions. Meanwhile, the downward pressure on prices caused by competition among existing firms and the entry of new firms into the market (limited if not impossible under regulated conditions) will compel enterprises to improve operating efficiency. This will spark new investment among firms that are vital and capable enough to undertake the outlays; it will also act as euthanasia for firms and industries that are inherently inefficient or historically outmoded. With market profitability now directing resource usage, the application of labor and capital in production operations will require efficient resource allocation. The artificial wages and job protections unions possessed in certain industries such as railroads and airlines will, of course, come to an end.

Meanwhile, bad business habits and indefensibly uneconomical managerial activities will cease under competitive operations. The old regulated industry mentality of avoiding anything that smacks of newness will have to be replaced by a more innovative and entrepreneurial managerial philosophy. The habit of counting on the regulatory agency or the government to bail out financially troubled firms through rate increases or direct subsidies, such as the rail industry long enjoyed, will end.

Under regulation, price discrimination was common. Usually referred to as "cross subsidization," it appeared whenever certain customers were, with regulatory encouragement, charged considerably in excess of costs for the same service that other customers received at less than cost. In the telephone industry, before the AT&T breakup, cross subsidies existed when long-distance charges were artificially inflated to underwrite losses on local service. The result was to discriminate against business customers primarily and in favor of most residential phone users. In this case, deregulation has meant higher prices for residential phone users (but lower prices for all long-distance users). As with airline pricing, ending cross subsidies produces winners and losers. Only the shortsighted will oppose ending official price discrimination, for unless actual costs are the major determinant of rates and prices, we are employing a pricing system that is inefficient *and* unfair.

Finally, of course, a market-directed system explodes the fiction of the public interest. The notion that some bureaucratic authority can determine a transcendent public interest and then act to implement it belongs more to the realm of metaphysics than to that of sensible economic reasoning. To return to our earlier discussion of the ICC and America's railroads, we might speculate that left to the dictates of a free market—and without an ICC—a national transportation mix might have emerged that would have allowed each transport mode to develop its inherent strengths. Instead of the artificial competition created "in the public interest" that pitted trucks and railroads against each other but provided no way of determining their relative efficiency, each form of transportation could have exploited its own advantages, dropping out of markets where it had none. The market is indeed the best determinant of the public's best interests.

Evaluating Deregulation to Date

The final test for the effectiveness of deregulation is not logic but actual performance, and here deregulation has proved an important spur to the American economy. A look at the record should be convincing enough.

The Airline Deregulation Acts of 1977 and 1978 were the first important efforts to dismantle a regulated cartel and return it to competition. Under these laws, air carriers were granted greater rate-making freedom and greater freedom of entry and exit from airline markets. Accordingly, the Civil Aeronautics Board (which went out of business in early 1985, the first major regulatory agency so abolished) allowed airlines to fly on a "first come, first served" basis to most American cities. The action ended the old, inefficient practice of granting virtual monopoly power to certain carriers over certain routes. As a result, dozens of old companies altered their routes (both expanding and contracting service on specific routes). At the same time, more than a score of brand-new long-distance carriers suddenly appeared. Meanwhile, the market, rather than the CAB, was allowed to determine most airline rates. The new approach brought most long-distance airfares down. Loss-producing routes were abandoned to new specialized commuter lines or fares were adjusted upward by the larger carriers to reflect real operating costs. The new market freedom allowed the airlines to price and operate according to actual supply-and-demand conditions and permitted passengers to enjoy the price benefits of competition.

Two years after the deregulation of the airlines, the Motor Carrier Act of 1980 brought gradual deregulation to the trucking industry (regulated by the ICC since 1930). Again the approach was the same: to allow greater freedom in rate making by individual truckers and the easing of entry restrictions into long-haul, interstate trucking. The benefits to the public came quickly. More than 5,200 new trucking firms entered the industry in the first eighteen months of deregulation; 20,000 new route applications were filed with the ICC; and average freight bills went down 10 to 20 percent.

In 1980, railroads were also given some relief from ICC control. In particular, they were freed to make most rate changes without prior ICC approval and were given permission to contract directly with shippers at less-than-market rates for long-term, bulk shipments. Previously, approval for rate changes had cost the railroads up to $1 billion a year as the ICC delayed adjusting rates for inflation, and special shipper-railroad contracts had been held to be an illegal form of rebating.

The gains from deregulation have not been limited to transportation. The deregulation of long-distance telecommunications has produced consumer savings and a more vibrant industry. In banking and finance, some restrictions have been lifted on branch banking, bank mergers, and overseas banking operations. There is more freedom to offer greater variety of financial options to customers. The elimination of artificial limits on the operations and functions of banks and other financial institutions (although more needs to be done here) has promoted increased competition among commercial banks, thrifts, credit unions, brokerage firms, and insurance companies in funds markets, raising investor earnings possibilities and lowering customer charges.

While "reregulators" will doubtless cite the 1980s savings and loan (or thrifts) crisis as proof that deregulation doesn't work, their criticism misses the target. The thrifts' difficulties were really due to the fact that they had been regulated (protected) for too long. The inability of some thrifts to adjust to a freer market was not the fault of the market. For the most part, the savings and loan crisis was the result of clearly fraudulent activities of some bankers who abrogated their fiduciary responsibilities. Indeed, these illegal actions were directly traceable to the government. Federal intervention since the 1930s on behalf of protecting depositors through deposit insurance has made it very easy for numerous bankers to shirk their own responsibility to protect their customers' funds. Appropriate legal action against fraudulent behavior—not more detailed regulation—is the remedy for theft.

Those who now see certain "shortcomings" with deregulation forget that the gains of market-directed economic activities are not possible without occasional risks. Avoiding such risks through regulation may produce a desired orderliness, but only at an exceptionally high cost. Overall, the economic costs of regulation impose a much greater burden on society than any risks associated with market competition.

THE LIBERAL ARGUMENT

Regulatory agencies are the logical outcome of the need to improve market conditions in certain industries. Direct regulation is not essential to all markets, but in certain cases—mainly where natural monopolies tend to develop or should be encouraged—regulation by government agencies can maximize the benefits to both the consumer and the affected industry. Antitrust action, as we have discussed, is employed in cases of conspiracy to attain a socially undesirable monopoly advantage in the market, but direct regulation is a ratification of monopoly power. In exchange for this recognized monopoly position, a firm submits itself to close political and economic supervision.

The "Rules" of Regulation

Under regulation, business firms are guaranteed certain rights. For example, their property rights are legally protected, and confiscation is not a serious possibility. They are entitled to receive reasonable prices and a fair rate of return on their capital. In the specific geographic area in which it operates, a regulated firm is given partial or total protection from competition. A firm can challenge in the courts any regulating decision made by the relevant commission.

Regulated firms also have certain obligations. Their prices and profits must not be excessive. Prices should be established that offer the greatest possible service without compelling a company to forfeit its capital through continuous losses. Moreover, the regulated firm must meet all demand at the established prices. Any change in the quantity or quality of service must be approved in advance by the regulatory agency. The final decision in such cases as petitions for abandonment of service must balance two conflicting objectives: the firm's operational benefits and the public interest. Finally, all regulated industries must be committed to high levels of performance with the highest possible standards of safety to the public. The key to regulation philosophy, developed over ten decades of experience and through sixteen independent agencies, is this: a balance of public and private (corporate) interests.

The Public Interest Revisited

The deafening roar of the Conservative crowd cheering on the recent drift toward deregulation has drowned out reason. While theoretical arguments are developed with considerable elegance to "prove" that regulation doesn't work and that a return to market competition for previously regulated industries would improve economic efficiency and well-being, the real issue has been papered over. What we have forgotten in our rush toward deregulation is to ask ourselves why Americans introduced the regulatory experiment in the first place. Surely regulation did not just happen accidentally. What, then, were its antecedents? It began with the long-held view that certain "public interest" objectives could never be well served in unregulated markets.

In the current rewriting of American economic history, Conservatives fail to recall that most ventures into regulation by independent regulatory commissions were not simply unconscious evasions of a market-dominated economy. A survey of previously or presently regulated industries shows that regulation evolved only after consistent evidence of market failure under conditions of competition.

The creation of the ICC in 1887 and its development of real regulatory power over the next twenty years came only after the excessive and irrational building of the American railroad network had brought about a cutthroat competition that destabilized the industry.

Periodically, bloody rate wars would break out among the giants as each tried to gain a larger share of the restricted transportation market. Consequently, there were frequent bankruptcies and breakdowns in service. Because of their critical place in the economy, as railroads went, so went the nation. Every major financial panic and recession after the Civil War—in 1873, 1884, and 1893—started with railroad bankruptcies. Attempts at private rate fixing and cartels, even before their unconstitutionality was established by the Sherman Antitrust Act, almost always failed. Even so, these expedients harmed farmers and other shippers. This, then, was the situation when the ICC was created in 1887. The free market operation of the rail industry could no longer be tolerated. This view was held widely by bankers, farmers, shippers, and railroad management.

Space does not permit a detailed description of the gradual elaboration of the ICC authority. It is sufficient to say that the initial limited powers of the commission over rate setting were enlarged to cover nearly all operations of railroads engaged in interstate commerce. Eventually all commercial surface transport enterprises came under ICC jurisdiction. The accretions of power in every case were responses to the failure of competitive market operations in the transport industry.

The story was similar elsewhere as public regulation was employed to offset a variety of problems rooted in an overly competitive economic system. The regulation of the airwaves in the 1920s by the FCC made it possible for radio listeners to interpret the chatter coming from radios. Competitive stations had operated without license or assigned frequencies and the public was ill-served. The building of the Federal Reserve System in 1914 (following passage of the Federal Reserve Act of 1913) came after a hundred years of unregulated and chaotic competition. Banks, usually operating with the skimpiest of reserves, showed a dangerous tendency to fall off into periods of panic, which in turn drove the nation into episodes of economic depression. The SEC was created in the 1930s after the overzealous actions of securities firms and banks had played a central role in the financial collapse of 1929.

The list of regulatory responses to the market failures of a purely free and competitive economy goes on and on. Regulation does not reflect a situation where the nation has not tried competition, but rather where it has been tried and found wanting, where the disadvantages of competition have shown themselves to be greater than the community wishes to shoulder. Conservatives attack the concept of "regulation in the public interest" without admitting that the public was badly served by an unreliable and frequently bankrupt transportation system, by dangerous if not fraudulent banking practices, by unscrupulous investment bankers and brokers, and by an unregulated use of the airwaves. When railroads fail and banks close or when unregulated energy prices close industries and chill homes, the nation is not simply faced with some "readjustment of markets" but with a threat to its very survival. Accordingly, it has been understood that certain basic sectors of the economy have responsibilities that go beyond private interest, that in fact serve a broader public interest even if they are privately owned. Europeans generally chose to deal with this conflict of interests by nationalizing or operating as public enterprises industries with broad public interest responsibilities. Public regulation was a less extreme response to this problem.

Another dimension of the "public interest" approach is the commitment to maintaining "universal service." Under this philosophy, regulatory agencies frequently employ cross subsidization to ensure that certain customers who might not otherwise have obtained service if charges were based solely on costs do in fact have reasonable service. Essentially, an ability-to-pay principle is applied, with those with greater carrying capacity subsidizing those whose costs are high but capacity to pay is low. So it was that rural rail and trucking services were subsidized by long-distance shippers and that elderly, fixed-income phone users had part of their costs paid by large corporations. To Conservatives, this is price discrimination, pure and simple; however, they make no attempt to explain how society's interests would be better served if small communities atrophy for lack of reasonably priced transportation or if low-income families are left without phone service.

Finally, on behalf of the public interest, it is appropriate for the government to act as an allocator of scarce resources. For instance, regulating prices and limiting exploitation of natural resources, with a view toward rationing their use, are appropriate public policy objectives that transcend any narrow profit interests.

To be sure, regulation in the public interest is not without its costs. The costs, however, are not really the alleged costs of inefficiency so frequently cited by Conservatives. They are the costs of creating market stability and equity that would not otherwise exist. Supplying reasonably priced phone service to all users may mean higher costs for some users. A safer banking system costs more to operate than a dangerously weak and speculative one. These costs are more than offset, however, by the long-run gains achieved for the entire society. Deregulation, meanwhile, stresses only the benefit of short-run savings (profits, really) from relaxing our concern for the public interest.

The Deregulation Balance Sheet

Deregulation as an effective economic policy is now over two decades old. Evidence is abundant enough to make an evaluation, and, contrary to the cheery Conservative assessment, it is not all that supporting.

In the transportation industries, the results are at best mixed. Railroads generally have benefited at the expense of the less efficient trucking competitors and of hundreds of communities that have lost rail service. Accordingly, some shippers—those able to use railroads—have gained, while others have lost. In the airlines industry, the early pricing benefits obtained by consumers under greater competition were quite temporary. Very quickly the opening of new routes and markets was followed by a wave of mergers that reduced the number of competing air carriers and consequently increased monopolistic control over passenger traffic at each of the major hub cities. Characteristically, airfares began to rise and passengers noticed a steady deterioration of service.

Although not the specific result of dismantling a regulatory agency but certainly the outcome of other public policies running in that direction, the breakup of AT&T does not stand out as a shining example of deregulatory success. The ending of cross subsidization translated directly into high and rising phone bills for virtually all residential customers. Meanwhile, the alleged benefits of competitive long-distance service seem lost in the confusion of phone bills and the selecting of one's long-distance carrier. Most average users of the telephone regularly report in opinion surveys that they feel costs have risen and service has declined since the breakup of Ma Bell.

The extent to which deregulation can produce truly catastrophic costs for society is best illustrated by the banking and finance industry. With thrifts freed in 1982 to compete with commercial banks and other financial intermediaries, they found themselves compelled to pay fairly high interest rates to attract funds. Indeed, the exceptionally high interest rates of the time would have caused problems regardless of deregulation. However, now freed of earlier restraints that confined the savings and loan activities almost exclusively to mortgage markets, thrifts ventured into high-return—and high-risk—lending. Loans to speculative real estate ventures, solar energy companies, windmill farms, and the like had very high failure rates in the early 1980s. Accordingly, many banks drifted toward and finally into bankruptcy.

With depositors' savings insured, government was obliged to "socialize" the costs of savings and loan zeal in seeking high-return investments. Some will argue that this was a unique situation, largely the result of government insulating financial institutions from market discipline by insuring their fiduciary responsibilities. However, it does not take an overactive imagination to consider that the socialization of deregulatory costs is not necessarily limited to financial markets. Should conditions resulting from deregulation demand it, government bailouts of airlines, telecommunication companies, and the like are not unthinkable.

Naturally enough, true believers in deregulation do not argue that it is government's responsibility to save failed enterprises, even if the failure is directly traceable to deregulation. The market, they will argue, does not ensure protection for inefficient firms, just as it does not ensure that everyone will get the service or the goods they want at the price they would *like* to pay. The apparent logic and detached fairness of free market arguments is always impressive in the abstract, when no particular firm or no particular service or consumer is in mind.

Of course, some criticisms of regulatory agencies—especially regarding their inflexibility in the face of changed economic and technological conditions and their habit of becoming too cozy with the very firms they regulate—are quite valid. Some regulatory agencies have outlived their usefulness. The passing of the ICC in 1996 was scarcely noticed by anyone. However, such deficiencies are correctable and are not causes for abandoning regulation altogether. At best, a reasoned and longer view of deregulation and its effects indicates that dismantling regulation machinery will provide us with an opportunity to reexperience old problems. Liberals see little benefit from having to learn again that unregulated capitalism produces serious market failures and imperfections that must sooner or later be offset by government intervention.

THE RADICAL ARGUMENT

History readily shows that the natural inclination of production-for-profit enterprises is to acquire as much price-making power as possible. Therefore, the long-term outcome of competition is invariably the development of some degree of monopoly power. Yet, monopolistic power is not always easily attained. It often requires enlisting the apparatus of the state in its behalf to be effective. Accordingly, public regulatory commissions were organized in the United States to ratify the existence of monopoly. Regardless of the intention of reformers who championed their development, regulatory agencies worked primarily on behalf of the industries they regulated. The creation of independent regulatory agencies and their performance do not support the Liberal claim that "public interest" is a major element in regulatory action. Neither do they support the Conservative charge that regulation has been "antibusiness."

Curiously, however, the deregulation movement also has advanced the objective of creating monopoly—but, of course, not in an obvious way. From a Radical perspective, the free market to regulation to deregulation (and recently) to "reregulation" oscillations in public policy toward business are not a cycle at all, as conventional economists suggest, but are variations on the same monopoly capitalist theme. Such an argument will be unfamiliar to many non-Radicals and may initially appear to be contradictory. To make the Radical position a bit clearer, we will examine one regulatory case in considerable detail rather than undertake a broad survey of American regulatory activities. The Interstate Commerce Commission's regulation of surface transportation in the United States is an excellent representative example.

Regulation as a Creature of Industry: The Case of the ICC

Progressive Era legislative and regulatory actions, rather than being single-minded efforts to "compromise" the differences of parties on either side of a particular market (as the then-current political rhetoric maintained), were really efforts to bring order to highly disrupted and overly competitive markets. But "order" was achieved on terms that supported the principles of private property and corporate profit seeking, terms that replaced competition with official recognition of limited monopolistic power and cartelization.

The ICC from its very beginning was an attempt to create an official cartel in rail transportation. This policy was steadily enlarged and elaborated on by the industry. Eventually, it also was applied to other modes of public transportation (buses, trucks, water carriers, and pipelines under the ICC and air carriers under the Civil Aeronautics Board). The development of the ICC was not a haphazard abandonment of high principles; it was the unfolding of a planned and rational policy. (It was rational at least in the sense that it consistently pursued clear ends, even though these goals might ultimately result in economic and social loss to the nation.)

Although many economic interests favored the creation of a federal railroad regulatory agency in the late 1880s, one of the most influential groups consisted of railroad leaders themselves. The closing decades of the nineteenth century had witnessed costly rate wars and other competitive difficulties, resulting largely from the enormous excess capacity built into the industry. These conflicts could not be handled through private efforts at cartelization, partly because these efforts usually collapsed of their own enforcement weaknesses and partly because other economic groups challenged such blatant attempts to build monopoly power. The railroads, therefore, turned to the federal government for official sanction of cartel creation. Progress toward this end began with passage of the Commerce Act of 1887; over the next twenty years, in the ICC and in Congress, railroads obtained important recognition as a cartel. Indeed, the Elkins Act (1903), which ended the hated competitive practice of paying rebates to certain shippers, was written in the legal offices of the Pennsylvania Railroad. The Hepburn Act (1906), which enlarged the ICC's power, supposedly at the expense of the rail monopolies, had considerable management endorsement.

"Community of interest" (informal domination of all rail operations in a region by a few large roads) and other plans formulated to integrate rail properties for the purpose of gaining greater monopoly power were frustrated for a time, but railroads emerged from World War I, after their ignominious operational collapse and more than two years of government control, with the Esch-Cummins Act of 1920. This law, as interpreted by the ICC and the courts, firmly established the principle of railroad cartelization. The old competitive situation within the industry no longer existed and the rail network was reduced to a limited number of essentially noncompetitive systems. Most state regulatory powers over finance and operations were abolished. The old ambition of industry pooling and rate bureaus was nourished during the Depression. Throughout the disastrous 1930s, the government, at Franklin Roosevelt's insistence, officially recognized the Association of American Railroads as the industrywide policy-making body. It was a powerful lobby and a tool for encouraging collusion within the industry. At the behest of rail leaders, the government moved in 1935 to control competition from the hated trucks and buses by placing them under ICC regulatory control. Finally, with the passage of the Transportation Act of 1940, the federal government officially declared an end to any pretense of maintaining "costly competition," either between railroads or among competing transport modes.

None of these regulatory and legislative successes by the railroads could, however, insulate the industry from competition or the structural and demand dislocations that persistently wreaked havoc with railroad balance sheets through the 1950s and 1960s. The decline was not halted even by the hastily drawn Transportation Act of 1958, which took away the last effective regulatory power of the states over passenger trains, nor by the ICC's growing willingness to approve almost any kind of merger or abandonment. The railroads had succeeded in getting themselves established as a protected cartel. Though they were not totally free to undertake whatever was in their interest, the official commitment to maintaining railroads as a privately owned industry meant that railroad legislation and regulation were loaded in their favor. The industry had to be kept going—on its own terms. For society, this translated into the reduction of rail service and the steady deterioration of service that remained.

The "Deregulation" Phenomenon

In many respects, the emergency legislation efforts to deal with the rail crisis in the Northeast corridor reveal the actual content, past and present, of our transportation and regulatory policy. Under the 1976 Regulatory Act, the six bankrupt northeastern railroads were organized into Conrail. Two points are noteworthy in this development. First, Conrail, although federally organized, was to become a private production-for-profit corporation after it had been reconditioned by a massive infusion of government funds and by a ruthless reduction in its trackage. Second, Conrail was devised to rescue the funds of the bankrupt railroads' investors. Although the initial government estimate of the scrap value of the bankrupt roads was set at $621 million, the owners claimed their deteriorated rolling stock and rusting rails to be worth at least $7 billion. Under pressure from banks, insurance companies, and other holders of railroad securities, Conrail was initially granted $2.1 billion in federal funds to acquire the nearly worthless financial paper of these roads. The prospects of monetary gain from Conrail were evident to the investors in the bankrupt lines, many of whom spoke glowingly of government ownership. There was little talk of such actions being "socialistic," but John Kenneth Galbraith has correctly called it "socialism for the rich."

The Motor Carrier Act of 1980 and the Staggers Rail Act of the same year put the finishing touches on what had been started four years earlier. The former deregulated trucking, and the latter gave broad rate-making and other freedoms to railroads. Deregulating surface transportation can only help the railroads, just as regulation helped in an earlier stage. With the end of ICC pricing strategies that protected the less efficient long-distance trucking industry, deregulation gives railroads a chance to utilize their major cost advantage over trucks. Regulation previously protected railroads from competition between themselves and the highly subsidized truckers. Now, with the railroad industry highly concentrated (and few new railroads likely to be built), intermodal competition will likely create rail domination of trucking. The less concentrated trucking industry is already feeling the effects as its profits fall and rail profits rise. In the railroad-truck competition, giant transportation firms can be built on the railroad stem as railroads expand trailer on flat car (TOFL) and container service on long-distance routes and add their own trucking facilities at either end of their rail routes. For a while there may be an illusion of competition (more truckers, more rate freedom, and so on), but the competition only masks the development of new monopoly power in the transportation industry.

The surface transportation industry scenario, which we have examined in detail, reflects the case of other industries undergoing deregulation. Among the deregulated airlines, despite the early appearance of new entrants in the market, recent mergers are increasing the likelihood of greater concentration among long-distance carriers. Caught up in the deregulation mood of the times, the Federal Communications Commission has permitted several giant mergers and a very large number of small ones in the radio and television industries. These mergers have narrowed the number of independently owned radio and television stations and created several absolute giants in broadcasting. Deregulation in banking has meant the building of giant "financial service" enterprises that combine banking and nonbanking functions as well as the enlargement of already huge banks by reducing restrictions on branch banking and interstate banking.

Such developments in no way support the Conservative claim that deregulation is restoring competition. Deregulation only continues the cartelizing of certain industries that commenced in the now discredited era of regulation.

Deregulation, whatever its immediate short-term gains to particular industries, can never be a long-term strategy. The destabilizing effects of excessive monopoly power—the direct result of deregulation—must be corrected to maintain economic and social order. The potential for abuse by deregulated but monopolistic railroads and air carriers provokes pressure for reregulation from the public and from commercial shippers. Similarly, the destabilizing of American banking and finance cannot be permitted. The banking industry requires reregulation to provide "orderly" financial markets. The recent appeal of controlling and cartelizing deregulated industries, while appearing to be a new public policy direction, is merely a return to the old strategy of creating officially protected cartels.

As deregulation pressures wind down and give way to calls for "reregulation," we should learn this lesson: *Social ownership and control of predominantly "public interest" industries offers the only viable alternative.* Public ownership and operation of transportation, banking, telecommunications, and the like is a means of establishing the collective control that regulation initially promised but could not achieve and that deregulation directly opposes.

Income Distribution

How Successful Will Our Experiment with Welfare Reform Be?

Like all other contracts, wages should be left to the fair and free competition of the market, and should never be controlled by the interference of the legislature.

The clear and direct tendency of the poor laws is in direct opposition to these obvious principles: it is not as the legislature benevolently intended, to amend the condition of the poor, but to deteriorate the condition of both poor and rich; instead of making the poor rich, they are calculated to make the rich poor.

David Ricardo, 1821

It is not to die, or even to die of hunger, that makes a man wretched; many men have died, all men must die. . . . But it is to live miserable we know not why; to work sore and yet gain nothing; to be heart-worn, weary yet isolated, unrelated, girt in with a cold, universal Laissez Faire.

Thomas Carlyle, 1853

A very substantial portion of poverty and unemployment is chronic, beyond the control of individuals or the influence of rising aggregate demand.

The President's Commission on Income Maintenance Programs, 1969

I don't see how taking my kids' welfare check away is going to help me find a job.

Chicago welfare mother, 1997

The Problem

In the fall of 1995, the House of Representatives passed legislation that would eventually convert the bulk of American welfare programs from direct federal control to "block grants" paid to and administered (under certain general federal guidelines) by the fifty individual states. It was the most momentous event in the past sixty years of American policy making in the area of public welfare administration. The block-granting of funds to the states seemed to many to mean the repeal of an old covenant between the federal government and the nation's needy that could be traced all the way back to the New Deal of Franklin Roosevelt. To others, it was less a reneging on an old promise than a matter of coming to terms, "getting real," with the mess the nation's welfare system had become.

That the welfare system was a mess was a matter about which both its defenders and its opponents could agree. Even the most ardent defenders of the patchwork system of transfer payments to needy citizens had difficulty defending the existing welfare arrangements. The system, even when working at its best, creaked along under a heavy and marvelously tin-eared bureaucracy. Reports of welfare cheating, as well as tales of manifest indifference to the problems of the truly needy, were regularly chronicled on the nightly TV news. And always the image of a welfare system from which its recipients never seemed able to escape loomed over the arguments of its defenders and opponents. Quite simply, something had to be done; and the block-grant strategy, coupled with requirements placing time limits on welfare eligibility and mandates for training the poor for jobs or, in any event, substituting "workfare" for "welfare" income, won the day. The federal program for providing welfare relief to "the deserving poor" ceased to exist as a citizen's right.

Welfare as a right was, in fact, a comparatively new idea in the United States. Its origins could not be traced back beyond the 1930s, and, some would argue, not really beyond the late 1960s. In the distant past (before the twentieth century), any "welfare" that existed was mostly provided by private charitable activity, sometimes by churches but most frequently by the largesse of compassionate friends and relatives. As late as 1902, combined federal, state, and local outlays for public welfare totaled only $41 million and practically all of this came from local governments. This amounted to 0.2 percent of GDP. Small wonder that one of John Dos Passos's characters in his novel about early twentieth-century America, *The 42nd Parallel* (1930), opined: "When you're out a luck in this man's country, *you're out a luck.*"

Until the 1930s, public assistance, such as it was, was always intended to address short-term instances of wagelessness or poverty. Commonly, the recipient was required to work at some public-sector job for the assistance received. Indeed, FDR followed that long-accepted pattern with his "make-work" WPA welfare programs in the 1930s.

In 1934, at the depths of the Great Depression, public welfare outlays by state, local, and federal governments totaled about $1 billion, or about 2 percent of the GDP. Still, public assistance was seen as a short-term phenomenon. Unlike Great Britain, where the poorhouse and the dole had persisted for more than a century as a way of life for the truly poor, no similar arrangements were constructed in the United States to deal with chronic poverty. However, the notion that citizens had a "right" to public assistance began to take shape with certain New Deal programs—Aid to the Aged, Aid to the Disabled, and Aid to Dependent Children (later to be known as Aid to Families with Dependent Children, or AFDC). In the late 1960s, President Lyndon Johnson's War on Poverty efforts left no doubt that access to public assistance was a right for all needy citizens.

By 1978, with the federal government having essentially taken control of most public assistance programs (although the states still exercised some influence over the level of certain in-state payments), means-tested (or income-based) public assistance programs accounted for over $63 billion in federal outlays and $20 billion in state outlays. Such programs included Medicaid, AFDC, Supplemental Security Income, Food Stamps, Child Nutrition, Housing Assistance and Opportunity Grants. By the mid-1990s, federal and state cash and in-kind assistance and Medicaid had grown to over $225 billion. Large as such a figure seems, it was still only a bit over 3 percent of GDP.

In any case, in the emerging debate about the nation's welfare program, the actual size of the public assistance outlay was always secondary to another question: What exactly was the nation buying with its welfare outlays? Even the welfare system's defenders took little pride in what had been created. True, by the mid-1990s, public assistance was only a temporary stopping spot for most of the 10 to 12 percent of the nation who were "poor"; but almost half of the poor, about one in every twenty Americans, were caught in "hard-core" poverty. Among this group, public assistance, for whatever reason, had become a permanent condition. And with this condition came all too frequently an ugly social pathology of broken families, unmarried mothers, educational failure, joblessness, high rates of substance addiction and crime, and, always, abiding personal despair.

In the 1990s, amidst an increasingly conservative political climate, the old American opposition to providing a permanent dole resurfaced with a vengeance. Politically speaking, there was no way to oppose the growing national will to abolish welfare as a "right" and to place stringent restrictions upon it as a privilege. The political mood was doubtless buoyed by the good economic times of the 1990s; people should be able to work themselves out of welfare, it was widely believed. It remains to be seen if this political outlook will endure, especially if the bright economic conditions begin to fade and the prospect for social disorder arises in a nation that has few safety nets for its poor.

Synopsis

Conservatives maintain a profound skepticism about the efficacy of social welfare programs, arguing that efforts at redistributing income are bound to produce a drag on economic performance. Liberals contend that a distribution of income based upon markets is bound to generate inequitable results that can be offset only through governmental manipulation of taxes and transfers. Radicals express deep-felt rejection of capitalism's exploitative mechanism of distributing economic rewards and would make a first step in rectifying matters through aggressive redistribution of income and wealth.

Anticipating the Arguments

- On what specific grounds do Conservatives condemn the view that welfare is "a right" that should be guaranteed to all needy citizens?
- While Liberals may agree with Conservatives that past uses of the welfare system have failed to help the poor, how do their proposals for dealing with poverty differ from the Conservative view?
- Radicals maintain that we have attempted to get rid of welfare support only for the needy but not for the well-to-do. What do they mean by such an assertion?

THE CONSERVATIVE ARGUMENT

From the perspective of American Conservatives, the contemporary dismantling of the nation's welfare system is an undertaking that is long overdue. Whatever the good intentions of several generations of welfare advocates, their efforts placed a heavy burden on the entire society, perhaps the heaviest of all on those citizens whom they sought to "help." The current shift in American social policy toward dismantling the dole and bringing the nation's poor and less fortunate population into the mainstream of economic life is to be lamented only because it took so long for common sense to be translated into actual practice.

The Sources of the "Welfare Problem"

The sources of modern America's welfare problem are not difficult to determine. They reside amidst the rubble of the general economic collapse of the 1930s—the Great Depression. Poverty, of course, did not make its first appearance in the 1930s; but, beginning in the 1930s, America began to institutionalize poverty. Heretofore in the American experience, poverty and the joblessness that was its primary cause had been viewed as a temporary experience. Moreover, it was an experience that, given time and the hard work of the poor themselves, the poor could sooner or later put behind them. Indeed, by the 1920s, the record was rather clear on this. Most of those who came to America voluntarily came poor and, within a generation or two, managed to escape the clutches of poverty. Only black Americans, devastated by their experiences first with slavery and then with agrarian sharecropping, moved out of poverty slowly. But even among this group of citizens on the eve of the Great Depression, there was noticeable upward economic movement.

Whether or not the Great Depression had to be as deep or prolonged as it was is a matter of debate. Conservatives, of course, hold the view that this great rupture in American political and economic life was really worsened by the Liberal response it initially brought forth. In any case, with unemployment hovering at about 25 percent, the matter of providing relief for the unemployed and the poor was an important underlying issue in the presidential contest that year between President Herbert Hoover and New York Governor Franklin D. Roosevelt. The Republican and philosophically conservative Hoover took the correct, but unpopular position, that any federal provision of emergency funds to the needy would establish a precedent that would eventually destroy the long-held American commitment to "individualism." FDR won and the die was cast for the growth of the American "welfare state."

Interestingly, even Roosevelt had reservations about establishing a permanent "womb to the tomb" welfare system. As late as 1935, a couple of years after introduction of his Works Progress Administration make-work relief program and his Aid to Dependent Children program, FDR observed: "The lessons of history, confirmed by evidence immediately before me, show conclusively that continued dependence upon relief induces a spiritual and moral disintegration fundamentally destructive to the national fiber. To dole out relief in this way is to administer a narcotic, a subtle destroyer of the human spirit. It is inimical to the dictates of sound policy. It is a violation of the traditions of America. Work must be found for able-bodied but destitute workers."

No Conservative could have stated the case any more forcefully than Roosevelt did. However, putting the toothpaste back in the tube was politically impossible. Once the Liberal solution to poverty—providing a dole for any who chose to demonstrate need—became understood as an American "right," it would not be a right quickly surrendered. The more so, of course, as the extent and amount of public relief continued to grow in the 1960s and 1970s. More than half a century would pass after FDR's public lament before a Conservative Congress could put an end to this awful Liberal experiment in social engineering.

Toward a Just System of Rewards

As the American welfare system grew, especially in the 1960s and 1970s, so did the notion that the nation would be better served with a more equal distribution of income. More than is generally realized, this idea legitimized the expansion of the welfare system and obscured real understanding of the terrible outcomes that welfare dependence was producing. Accordingly, it is important at this point to understand where Conservatives stand on the entire matter of income distribution before taking up the particular issue of current welfare reform.

A unifying feature of all Liberal and Radical programs for the past hundred years has been the call for egalitarianism in income. The "Robin Hood" illusion is the very beginning of any collectivist's social dream. In the United States, income redistribution efforts in this century have appeared in two general forms: (1) a highly progressive income tax structure aimed at piling the expense of social spending on the upper-income elements of society, and (2) a vast giveaway of these appropriations to the poor and the nonproductive groups within the nation. Both schemes rest on serious errors of economic and social thinking that deserve fuller elaboration and criticism.

Distribution of income should be governed by the simple and equitable principle that all members of a society should receive according to what they, or whatever they own, are able to produce. The abilities, tastes, and occupational interests of individuals vary. People value work and leisure differently. Some individuals are willing to forgo an assured lower income in favor of taking a risk and possibly earning more. Enforced equality of income utterly fails to consider these possibilities. It presumes that greater social satisfaction is attained by income parity rather than by letting people make their own valuations of what money means to them.

Consider, for instance, a person who is quite content to live on $100 a week. From this person's point of view, needs are satisfied and the right balance between leisure and work has been achieved. To transfer to this person one-quarter of the wages of another person who makes $500 a week will hardly increase the first person's welfare or happiness. At the same time, it subtracts much satisfaction from the second person, who is willing to work hard enough to earn the $500 wage. If we now added up the relative satisfactions of the two workers, it would be lower after redistribution than before. In other words, proof is lacking that a more equal income distribution actually maximizes community satisfaction.

At another level, egalitarianism leads to more serious troubles. Enforcing equal distribution of income penalizes the industrious and inventive and subsidizes those with less initiative. If the industrious fail to obtain rewards for their talents and work, they will naturally slacken their efforts. As a result, the total productiveness of society is lessened. In the subsequent egalitarian redistribution, everyone gets less than before. Just how far the detrimental effects of income equalization can go in destroying a society became evident in Great Britain by the 1970s. Subsidies for nonproduction and confiscation of earned income had lowered British output and put the nation at considerable disadvantage in world trade. The best minds and the nation's capital were fleeing overseas. At home, there was a shabby equality as well as mediocrity. Only the reversal of the old welfare-state policies by the Conservative government of Margaret Thatcher in the late 1970s and early 1980s saved Britain from social and economic collapse.

While the discussion so far has been mostly concerned with individual labor, it also applies to individuals' command over capital and wealth. Appropriating the wealth of one person to support another denies the individual's right to property and will lead to inefficiency and economic contraction in the whole society. (Whether the wealth is inherited or has been earned by the individual is irrelevant.) This is not just an economic matter. Seizures of wages and property are violations of freedom. It is not such a big step from telling people what their income will be to telling them what work to do or what ideas to think.

The Basic Problems with Welfare

Conservatives have long understood that their attack upon welfare is often depicted as a Scrooge-like heartlessness. In a nation of abundance and opportunity, it is natural that there should be much popular support for charity for the "deserving poor." But charity involves a number of costs.

First of all, there is the cost to the "giver." In the growing national economy of the 1960s, the expansion of a variety of welfare programs— AFDC, for example—provoked little taxpayer response. The programs seemed relatively small and, enjoying an impressive annual growth rate in the nation's gross domestic product, few Americans doubted that this was a charity we would someday not be able to afford. However, in the slower-growth 1990s, a lot of working Americans began believing that charity should start at home. No doubt this self-concern was sharpened by the new realities of American labor markets. Corporate downsizing meant many American workers had to take considerable pay cuts as they scrambled about for new jobs. In the new employment environment, a growing friction emerged between those choosing to work, even at considerably reduced wages or with the prospect of reduced wages, and millions of welfare recipients choosing not to work at all. That the former should continue to support the latter comfortably made less and less sense to many hard-working citizens. By the mid-1990s, public opinion polls no longer indicated that the majority of Americans supported the nation's welfare experiment.

There was also growing recognition of a second type of cost that welfare exacted, this one borne by its recipients. Aid to Families with Dependent Children, given only to mothers and children in the absence of a working father, was from its very beginning—although well-intended welfare advocates generally ignored the fact—constructed so as to fracture the families of the poor. It also encouraged out-of-wedlock childbirth. Accordingly, millions of children were denied the opportunity to grow and thrive within a conventional nuclear family. Generally, cash-assistance welfare programs required that eligible recipients have no earned income or that any earned income be subtracted from welfare payments received.

The overall effect of America's welfare program is easily summarized: It has created a strong disincentive to work and always has discouraged people from improving themselves. Recipients not only have had to be poor to qualify for welfare protection, but they have had to endeavor to stay poor to keep getting it. Thus our welfare system created a vast, permanent subculture of the disadvantaged. And, of course, overseeing this mess was a monumental welfare bureaucracy utterly lacking in incentives to "solve" the welfare dilemma, since their very paychecks depended on the problem's continued existence. It is hard to imagine that such an irrational system could have been defended, and thereby have been permitted to exist, for so many years.

Thoughts on Welfare Reform

For most Conservatives, the recent efforts at welfare reform are only a beginning. Returning the administration of the welfare system to the states via "block grants" is useful for a couple of reasons. First, it is a beginning step in the breaking up of the national welfare bureaucracy; and second, states are best able to develop and administer programs that respond to regional welfare needs.

Meanwhile, shifting the emphasis of welfare administration from "welfare" to "workfare" acknowledges an important fact: Welfare is not a categorical "right" conferred by citizenship or membership in this society. It is, at best, a privilege, and even when conferred carries with it a quid pro quo requirement. Even Conservatives understand that circumstances may arise from time to time that make it impossible for some citizens to find work. To the extent that an individual is disabled and unable to work at all or is too young to work, we recognize that society bears a responsibility to provide for the basic needs of those so affected. But when an individual is capable of working, it is not a cruel act by society to require that person to provide some useful labor on behalf of those providing his or her support.

With regard to current welfare-reform efforts to encourage recipients to find private sector employment, Conservatives are particularly enthusiastic. Restoring a sense of self-worth to former welfare recipients by means of their finding jobs is really the only long-term cure for the welfare problem. However, and this is an important point to keep in mind, successfully engaging former welfare recipients in the ordinary economic life of the nation requires more than a little job training here and a little career counseling there. As a nation, we should be very careful that some of our economic initiatives, often actions that seem to have nothing to do with the "welfare problem," do not work against solving that problem. For instance, the simple act of raising the legal minimum wage may seem to many to be a fairly benign undertaking aimed only at raising the living standards of a few million low-wage workers. In fact, such an action, or any others that raise an employer's cost in hiring additional workers, will shrink the employment opportunities of current welfare recipients and may even be the cause of a new round of joblessness and a resurgence of the old welfare cycle.

Remember, from a Conservative perspective, welfare dependency emerged in the first place as the result of undesirable tinkering with a market economy. We can "reform" welfare as much as we like, but the usefulness of such reforms depends ultimately on our commitment to permitting the economy to operate freely and openly, with as little social and economic interference as possible.

THE LIBERAL ARGUMENT

Conservatives are on the right track when they attack redistributive programs, but not for the reasons they present. The failure of public policy efforts is not due, as Conservatives believe, to some collectivist utopia in which a massive Robin Hood program takes from the rich and gives to the poor, simultaneously trampling on property rights, reducing work incentives, and lowering overall economic efficiency and national economic growth. Liberals maintain that public policy actually *has* failed in its professed efforts to close the gap between those at the very bottom of the income distribution and those at the top.

Conservatives are by no means troubled by this aspect of public policy failure and indeed perceive inequality as in some measure incentive-inspiring and a *normal outcome* of well-functioning competitive markets. Liberals question the disincentives and adverse effects upon economic growth that Conservatives purport to be the by-products of the oversized welfare state. Moreover, the Liberal view challenges the ability of the market mechanism to generate socially acceptable results with regard to income distribution. Conservatives turn a blind eye to the potential contagion of social problems that accompany poverty. We criticize Conservatives' methods of reforming welfare as overridingly motivated by the goals of reducing the influence of central government and curtailing redistribution under the guise of *cost savings*—all the while chanting the popular mantra of *efficiency*.

Liberals are receptive to reforms that reduce costs and improve efficiency but are realistic in our evaluation of income distribution and the limitations upon economic opportunity that poorly functioning markets are bound to impose. Consequently, while adhering to the notion of personal responsibility and self-reliance, Liberals maintain that government's role in welfare can never be as small as Conservatives would hope.

The Facts of Income Distribution

As Table 6.1 illustrates, shares of money income received by various American income groups showed some movement toward greater equality in the New Deal era of the 1930s. The distribution was markedly stable from the 1940s to the mid-1970s. Thereafter the distribution began to exhibit greater inequality. Moreover, the quintile figures

Table 6.1

Share of Aggregate Income Received by Families in Each Income Quintile, 1929–1994

Income quintile	1929	1936	1947	1960	1970	1980	1987	1994
Lowest	—	4.1	5.0	4.8	5.4	5.1	4.6	4.2
Second	12.5*	9.2	11.9	12.2	12.2	11.6	10.7	10.0
Third	13.8	14.1	17.0	17.8	17.6	17.5	16.8	15.7
Fourth	19.3	20.9	23.1	24.0	23.8	24.3	24.0	23.3
Highest	54.4	51.7	43.0	41.3	40.9	41.6	44.0	46.9

Source: U.S. Census Bureau.
*Lowest and second quintile combined.

mask the fact that the share of income going to the top 5 percent climbed from under 16 percent in the 1970s to over 20 percent by the middle of the 1990s. Initially, it has been difficult to determine whether this is a passing episode or a change in the long-term trend of the distribution of income. Some would say it is still too early to tell. Regardless of which position one prefers to take, the facts are that the economic situation of those persons at the bottom of the distribution has not appreciably improved. Throughout the same time period, individuals in the highest quintiles in the income distribution were claiming an even larger share of money income. Clearly, such evidence does not support the Conservative suggestion that we have been on a long and dangerous slide toward egalitarianism.

Liberals concede that the sources of the rise in income inequality are numerous and elusive. Experts cite the impact of technological change that has handsomely rewarded particular types of skills, adverse effects of international competition that happened to be more pronounced for the inhabitants of the bottom of the income distribution, decline in the purchasing power of the minimum wage, lower levels of unionization in the labor force and weakening of union influence over wages, and an influx of low-skill, low-wage immigrants who shrink the income share figures at the bottom of the distribution. However, these explanations have little to do with the Conservative assault upon government's efforts to redistribute income via the welfare system. And despite these explanations one must bear in mind that the principle focus of redistributive efforts has not been to significantly alter the distribution of income. Specifically, the evolution of welfare programs has been a response to the inadequacies of a market system and the experiencing of the actual consequences of those inadequacies.

Belief Versus Reality

In its strictest embodiment, the Conservative view has a terribly difficult time reconciling the predictions of its most honored models with actual phenomena. This is particularly true when models of competitive markets are compared against real-world results. While acknowledging that theoretical models of *perfect* markets suffer from a strained relationship with their real-world counterparts, Conservatives are reluctant to acknowledge that the problems of monopoly power, the absence of complete information—or the presence of distorted information—for consumers to make intelligent choices, and the serious failures of markets (as in the case of pollution) are serious enough to warrant much intervention on the part of government. Likewise in the cases of poverty and income inequality, Conservatives are unwilling to find the justification for government intervention.

Experience finds this perplexing. The depths of the Great Depression motivated a fiscally and ideologically conservative President Franklin Roosevelt to discard Conservative claptrap in favor of *Liberal* policies that might at the very least *finesse* the problem. Similarly, the enviable, burgeoning production economy of the United States was tormented in the post–World War II period by a legacy of high poverty rates in excess of 20 percent. These rates began to fall with the onset of a combination of economic growth and redistributive policies—both instilled through government intervention—that improved the economic lot for not only the citizenry from the bottomland of the income distribution but all else as well. On the subject of economic growth, both Conservatives and Liberals agree: The best way out of poverty is a job. However, the contingency is *economic growth*. Here, as on other matters, Liberals must part company with the Conservatives.

The Basis for Intervention

Although the landscape of reasons is expansive and can become highly detailed, the Liberal argument for intervention and income maintenance programs rests mainly upon the following foundations:

- that competition in markets is not universal and the existence of monopoly power and other market imperfections necessitates government corrective action on several fronts, including redistribution of income;
- that private markets fail and cannot insure people against the uncertainty of economic downturns that throw people out of work and into poverty;
- that egalitarianism is not at odds with economic growth;
- that government policies should be crafted to fight poverty and promote fairness in the income distribution—not just to unload or shift around the financial burden of paying for the nation's poor.

Market Imperfections

Theories of competitive product markets and resource markets presume certain ideal conditions that dodge practical complications and establish something of a "fair game." Conservatives maintain that such models strongly represent economic reality and Radicals reject them outright. Liberals reside in between with well-founded concerns about the magnitude of imperfections in real-world markets. These imperfections are bound to influence the fairness of the game and, therefore, the fairness of the results. Recognize that Conservatives do not perceive imperfections as a very large problem and Radicals believe the game is rigged.

Obviously, since the competitive model of Conservative yesteryear is countered by the existence of monopoly power in product markets, the results must be reflected in the income distribution. In short, the monopolist gets rich at the expense of society as whole.

Likewise, labor markets routinely exhibit inequality in bargaining power between employer and employee in determining wages, with the employee in the weaker position. Other imperfections in the form of geographic and sociological immobilities impair the performance of labor markets by denying people ready access to improved economic opportunities just because they are unaware, too far away, or can be had only after insurmountable personal adjustments. Other citizens experience lack of opportunity and access to proper education, training, and experience—what economists call *human capital*. Hence, insufficient investment in human capital yields paltry returns in the form of income earned in the labor market, which in turn leads back to low investment, trapping the poor in a vicious circle of poverty.

Poverty and inequality are further cultivated by circumstances that are beyond the control of individual choices and relative efforts in labor market. Some may suffer from the limitations imposed by disabilities. Others are the victims of accidents and misfortune. Still others must tangle with labor market discrimination. Certainly society could not be intent upon ignoring or punishing these people.

Welfare as Social Insurance

Conservatives are well aware that economic activity for certain sectors of the economy would be greatly retarded or nonexistent were it not for the development of insurance. Insurance offsets the discouraging effects imparted by random accidents, bad weather, fire, flood or other adverse events where, based upon past experience, an insurer can estimate the expected frequency and severity with which such events will occur. Private insurance functions quite well within a particular domain. However, private insurance markets do not provide adequate (or any) insurance against the uncertainties of the business cycle and consequent unemployment. Nor have private insurance markets found it financially feasible to extend coverage to the chronically ill or to develop income security insurance for low-wage workers with spotty employment histories. The development of social insurance programs, including antipoverty programs, is a response to this particular failure of markets.

Egalitarianism, Incentives, and Growth

Liberals do not subscribe to the same reasoning as Conservatives concerning the connection between income redistribution and economic incentives, and their attendant impact upon economic growth. At base the assertion that taxes levied upon productive efforts and transferred to unproductive individuals are a disincentive to being productive seems to make sense. This proves to be a matter of degrees or, perhaps more properly, *thresholds* at which extremely high taxes and bountiful welfare benefits truly discourage work effort, saving, and investment. In any event, there is no discernible, systematic relationship to support the idea that greater equity is accompanied by a pronounced loss of economic efficiency. Many European countries engage in far more vigorous tax and transfer efforts than the United States. Yet this does not seem to impinge upon economic progress. In fact there is merit to the argument that greater economic security improves the outlook for economic growth. By contrast, examples abound, primarily among less developed countries, of highly unequal distributions of income that are coupled with marked inefficiency and abysmal records of economic growth. Indeed, income redistribution does confront society with a dilemma. However, the trade-off is not so pointed that we must agonize about whether future economic growth is dangerously jeopardized by trying to help the poor.

Throw Them Overboard?

Liberals advocate that government policies should be designed to fight poverty and promote an equitable distribution of income. This overarching objective is not an obstruction to exploring the most expeditious and inexpensive means of dealing with the poverty problem. However, Conservative prescriptions for cost cutting and efficiency are worrisome. When likened to the allegorical overcrowded lifeboat, Conservative policies seem bent upon shrinking the size of the boat and heaving passengers overboard.

Although the Conservative agenda may be honestly dominated by the desire to shrink government and its influence, there is a certain mean-spiritedness to their methods. Liberals are, therefore, skeptical of efforts that merely shift the responsibility for, and burden of, the poverty problem from one level of government to another. Historical experience with the failure of "poor laws" that held local governments accountable for providing for their resident indigents is instructive: The approach was to make it legally difficult to be poor *and* be a resident, or for governmental provision for the poor to be parsimonious. The purpose of this strategy was to chase the undesirables into some other political jurisdiction where tolerance and provision for the poor was greater.

Inequities are certain to grow if each state establishes its *social minimum.* In the 1930s, some states denied voting rights to those on public assistance. In the 1950s, "welfare in some Mississippi townships consisted of $75 and a one-way bus ticket to Detroit." Inevitably, local governments would be prompted to adopt in common the worst of restrictions and frugality lest they be overwhelmed by legions of paupers. From this understanding of the problem of ceding responsibil-

Figure 6.1. **Poverty Rates, 1959–1996**

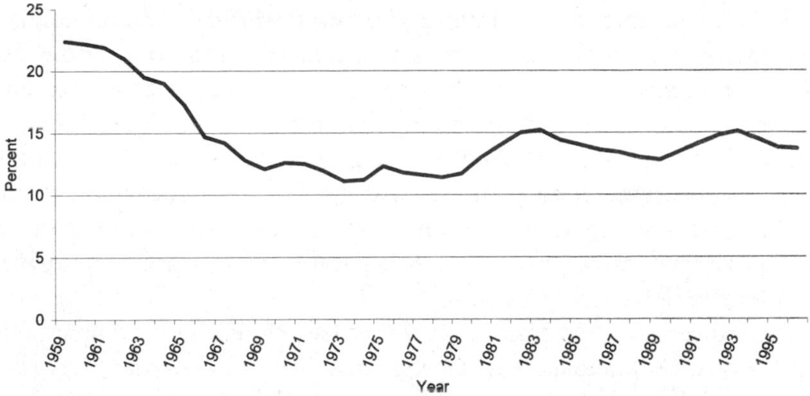

Source: Data from U.S. Census Bureau, *Historical Poverty Tables—Persons.*

ity to local authority emerges caution about policy reforms—especially if they reverse decades of progress in reducing poverty.

Success in Reducing Poverty Rates

Figure 6.1 shows the trend in poverty rates since 1959. There are some cyclical ups and downs because poverty rates rise during economic contractions and fall during periods of prosperity. The rate of economic growth is clearly a powerful force in determining poverty rates. A rising tide of economic growth lifts all boats—or nearly all. Conservatives are fierce advocates of work rather than welfare. However, this is most workable only when the economy performs well enough to provide sufficient employment opportunities. Even then, growth has never been a foolproof remedy for poverty and income inequality.

The 1960s brought the onset of expanded social insurance programs, and with impressive results. Propelled by President Lyndon Johnson's vision of the Great Society, poverty rates took a nosedive from over 22 percent of the population to slightly over 11 percent by 1973. Much of the improvement can be attributed to more generous Social Security benefits and the creation of Medicare in 1965, providing medical and hospitalization insurance to the aged. A companion program, Medicaid, was also initiated to pay the health care costs of the indigent. Social Security, Medicare, and even Medicaid, to the extent that it pays for nursing home and home health care for the elderly, have escaped the notoriety of being *welfare*. The beneficiaries, many of Conservative persuasion, fervently refuse to allow that *they* and *their* transfer payments from government bear any resemblance to the recipients of payments from Aid to Families with Dependent Children (AFDC) or Food Stamps. While older Americans could claim victory in the War on Poverty, beginning in the 1970s poverty rates rose at an alarming rate for persons under 18. Poverty continued to exhibit disparate impacts upon minorities and female household heads.

Nonetheless, the overall poverty problem would be far worse without government redistribution programs. In the *Economic Report of the President, 1997,* the president's Council of Economic Advisors estimates that cash transfer payments held the official poverty rate in 1995 to 13.8 percent; otherwise, it would have been 21.9 percent! Furthermore, the effect of the Earned Income Tax Credit (EITC—discussed below) and the value of *in-kind* transfers (such as subsidized housing and health care services) effectively reduce the poverty rate to 10.3 percent.*

The Liberal Agenda

The Liberal agenda for addressing the problems of poverty and income inequality is not based upon attempting to preserve the "welfare state" or the welfare bureaucracy. Rather, Liberals are guided by sound principles of where and when government should intervene as well as the desire for a humane and civil society. Let us translate that into a plan of action.

Increase the Minimum Wage

A straightforward way to raise income and encourage work is to raise the minimum wage. Policy makers need to revisit minimum wage legislation more frequently than every seven to nine years or index the minimum wage so that it automatically rises with consumer prices or in tandem with other wages in the economy.

Economic Report of the President, 1997, p. 186.

Maintain and Expand the Earned Income Tax Credit

The Earned Income Tax Credit permits low-income families to receive as much as 40 percent of earned income as refundable tax credit depending upon family size. The EITC is a version of a guaranteed annual income (GAI) or negative income tax (NIT) for the working poor. Even Conservatives like Milton Friedman have advanced some support for a GAI or NIT. The EITC is not a full remedy, but it has proven useful in offsetting poverty and reducing income inequality.

Fostering Economic Opportunity and Personal Responsibility

Welfare is not the real solution to poverty or income inequality. Programs designed to pacify the poor create a permanent poor. Federal programs must attack the root of the problem through job creation, training, and education. Although Liberals are not fully enthralled with "workfare" as an alternative to unrestricted grants to the poor, it is the only viable long-run strategy for eliminating chronic poverty. It is important to realize that success requires the cooperation of private enterprise for able-bodied people to make the transition from welfare to work.

The Liberal program requires devoting additional resources to the pursuit of eliminating poverty. Not all of these resources need to be marshaled by government. Government will intervene where such intervention is economically justified and can be expected to yield improvements. However, private enterprise cannot sit idly by regarding this social problem as principally a problem for government to solve. Private business professes a strong interest in reforming welfare and must therefore recognize that it is a quintessential partner to that end. Alas, Liberals must plead guilty to the Conservative charge that they would engage in social engineering, *but there is no other way.*

THE RADICAL ARGUMENT

The welfare "reform" bill that was recently passed by Congress and signed into law by President Clinton codifies and culminates a brutal attack that has been waged by the Right Wing on the poor and working class of America. Conservatives have been phenomenally successful in implementing their agenda to criminalize poverty and stigmatize the poor in order to eliminate any and all remaining social protections such as unemployment insurance and Social Security. While Senate and House Republicans are unabashed and unapologetic about implementing these changes, Liberals are somewhat more cautious regarding their likely success. Nevertheless, both view poverty as a *personal* failure of character or circumstance. To the Conservative, low incomes or the absence of any income at all reflect the market-determined value of an individual's talents and initiative: Defects of character and skill of the poor themselves are the root cause of their poverty. To the Liberal, poverty is partly the result of failing to behave in an economically responsible manner and partly the result of forces outside an individual's direct control such as racial discrimination, insufficient education, or other characteristics. Conservatives, of course, are content to let the poor struggle out of their condition, whereas Liberals are quick to apply moderately redistributive tax and transfer programs and other social-policy bandaids for the economically "disadvantaged." By focusing only on the personal characteristics of the poor, albeit in different ways, neither Conservatives nor Liberals recognize that poverty and extreme income inequality are inherent outcomes of the capitalist system.

Demoting the General Welfare

The debate over welfare reform has been almost entirely defined and discussed in profoundly moral terms. Poverty is generally assumed by both Conservatives and Liberals to be the result of an individual's inability to adopt market-friendly habits and attitudes, rather than the persistent failure of an economy that is equally proficient at producing extreme wealth *and* destitution. The new welfare law, or Personal Responsibility and Work Opportunity Act of 1996, began by noting that "Marriage is the foundation of a successful society," and then went on to blame the growth in poverty, crime, and general social decay since the 1960s on the increase in single motherhood. Left unchallenged was any notion that the lack of employment opportunities and financial resources causes crime and poverty rather than the reverse. Nor did the legislation acknowledge that white, married-couple families were twice as numerous among the poor as families led by a black, single mother. Politicians find it much easier to moralize about the sanctity of marriage than to acknowledge the crushing impact that their so-called "welfare reform" will have on the economic prospects of the poor.

While much attention has also been focused on the elimination of the Aid to Families with Dependent Children (AFDC) program, most of the projected spending cuts will come from reductions in other programs such as Food Stamps, Supplemental Security Income for the elderly and disabled, and assistance to *legal* immigrants. The AFDC Program—now renamed Temporary Assistance to Needy Families (TANF)—will be disbursed as block grants by the federal government to individual states. Welfare has now been formally transformed from a federally mandated entitlement—meaning that anyone who qualified for the program was admitted—to a discretionary benefit that states may offer their indigent citizens. States are allowed to impose their own restrictions and eligibility criteria and can even use the federal funds for other purposes. The only major federal restriction is that states are prohibited from granting benefits to families for more than five years. Not only has the federal government succeeded in abrogating its responsibility to guarantee some minimum standard of living for *all* its citizens, but states can now balance their budgets on the backs of the poor as they continue to cut social spending with impunity.

Under the guise of getting the incorrigible and indigent to adopt labor market–friendly behaviors and attitudes, "workfare" will mainly serve as a punitive function to lower overall wages and working conditions and break the power of organized workers. By 2002, the federal TANF program mandates that half of all single-parent adults and 90 percent of two-parent families will have to be working thirty hours per week. Since areas of high unemployment tend to also have high poverty rates, states will most likely seek to comply with the federal workfare requirements by firing their permanent workers and replacing them with TANF recipients. In places like New York City, this means a possible addition of 100,000 workers—equivalent to just under half of the current number of total municipal employees. For example, most of the 21,000 workfare placements in New York City as of March 1996 were in "maintenance" positions, primarily at the Parks Department, Department of General Services, and Sanitation Department. Furthermore, with workfare wages set at about one quarter of the full-time wage rate, there will be an irrepressible incentive for the city to get rid of its unionized municipal workers. The cumulative impact of these policies is clear: Millions of the poorest families in America will suffer under much worse conditions than they are presently living. Fewer than half of the expected 11 million affected families will be single mothers, and over half will be *working* families.

While workfare is clearly an attack on the poorest citizens, it also serves to undermine the wages, benefits, and employment conditions of all American workers. By destroying the economic safety net for those at the bottom, welfare reform has ensured that low-wage workers will remain docile with respect to demands for higher compensation and organizing activities. Even higher-paid workers will lower their expectations about pay and job security as they watch workfare recipients replace unionized workers. The Economic Policy Institute estimates that to absorb all the new workers, the wages of the bottom third of the labor force will have to fall about 10 percent nationally, and about 20 percent in urban areas with high rates of unemployment.

In sum, the pacification of the American poor and working class is just one of many consequences of the new welfare reform bill. These changes are not just about economics and government efficiency, they are also about exploiting antagonisms among and between the working poor and middle classes, between whites and "minorities," and about male power over women. Ultimately, this program will serve to polarize and immiserate American society, while consolidating and expanding the power of the corporate elite and their minions.

The Legacy and Reality of Wealth Inequality

Reforming the welfare system only serves to draw attention away from the fundamental problem of capitalism's inability to produce an equitable distribution of market outcomes. Adam Smith believed that, since growth was an intrinsic feature of capitalism, over time the rewards of the market would spread throughout the economy. While Smith recognized the potential for social conflict, he claimed that competition would prevent the concentration of economic resources and political power. Marx, who very much admired Smith's analysis of capitalism, agreed that capitalism was the only social system capable of generating unparalleled growth; however, it also produced unmatched poverty and inequalities in wealth and income.

While growth in aggregate income, output, and employment has been touted as a long-term feature of American capitalism, inequality in wealth and personal income has also persisted. In fact, with the exception of the early colonial era (through about 1800) and the periods during and around world Wars I and II, American society has been fairly polarized with respect to the distribution of both income and wealth. Although the Depression of the 1930s ushered in a time when incomes at the bottom and middle classes actually rose, since the mid-1960s inequality has steadily increased. Not only do mainstream economists regard this as necessary to spur personal initiative and corporate investment, but each year the business press gloats over the richest people in America. For example, *Forbes* magazine compiles a list of the 400 wealthiest people in America. In 1997, you needed a net worth of at least $474 million to qualify ($5 billion would have placed you only in the twentieth position). The United States currently has an estimated 170 billionaires while more than 36 million people languish in lives below the official poverty line (in 1996) of $15,911 for a family of four. In addition, since 1982, when the combined net worth of the *Forbes* 400 was "only" about $92 billion, that figure has now increased almost sevenfold to a net worth of about $624 billion. Finally, it should be noted that rather than being a bunch of Horatio Algers or self-made billionaires, a significant number of the *Forbes* 400 inherited most of their wealth.

While these figures only illuminate the wealth of the super-rich, it is quite evident that the overall distribution of wealth and income remains highly unequal. The following table provides data on the distribution of wealth, debts, and income based on the Federal Reserve's *Survey of Consumer Finances* for 1995. As Marx would have guessed back in the late nineteenth century, wealth is far more concentrated than income in capitalist America: While the bottom 90 percent garnered a little more than two-thirds of total income, it held only one-third of total wealth. Moreover, while their net worth was only slightly greater than their income, for the top 10 percent it was more than ten times as great.

The data also show that the top 10 percent—about 10 million households—owned 84 percent of stocks and 90 percent of bonds (either directly or as part of a mutual fund). On the other hand, it is painfully obvious that the vast majority of Americans have nearly all their assets in a home or car—resources that are not easily deployable to either capital markets or a new business. In fact, the top tenth of households owned over 92 percent of assets held in the form of businesses and well over two-thirds of real estate and other assets.

Table 6.2

Distribution of Assets, Liabilities, Income, and Net Worth*

	Bottom 90%	Top 10%
Assets	37.9	62.1
Home	66.4	33.6
Automobiles	77.6	22.4
Bonds	9.7	90.2
Stocks	15.6	84.4
Liabilities	70.9	29.1
Home mortgage	78.4	21.6
Other real estate	25.2	74.7
Other liabilities	80.6	19.4
Net worth	31.5	68.4
Income	$33,273	$ 134,933
Average net worth	$39,252	$1,217,375

Source: Federal Reserve Bank, Survey of Consumer Finances, 1995.
    *Figures are percentage shares except where dollar amounts are indicated. Percentage shares may not sum to 100 percent because of rounding.

Rather than an evolution toward a more democratic economy the data underscore how a small class of elites increasingly controls the financial resources that will determine the future livelihoods of most Americans. Moreover, while most of the rich were raised in wealth, more than one of five American children continue to grow up in poverty. In 1969, when the official poverty rate more accurately reflected the reality of the poorest citizens, the overall child poverty rate was only 14 percent. Not only does poverty deprive children of a decent standard of living, it also cuts their lives short. Despite our position as the world's wealthiest country, the United States ranks twenty-sixth in the mortality rate for children under five years of age. Not only do poor children have a much greater likelihood of dying from diseases and accidents, but even as adults, their longevity is likely to be curtailed by inadequate access to health care.

While welfare "queens" are vilified in the media, little attention is paid to the fact that social service expenditures also subsidize the rich and well-to-do. Welfare dollars buy the goods and services of corporate America. They underwrite the medical–industrial complex that

includes hospitals, doctors, drug companies, health maintenance organizations, and a host of suppliers and providers. For example, Medicaid fraud is almost always committed by doctors, hospital
administrators, insurance companies, and other well-paid health care
professionals. Rarely does an indigent patient ever benefit from such
crime. In fact, government expenditures on the truly needy (where
income eligibility tests are required) are a little more than 5 percent of
total federal outlays and have been steadily declining for several years.
Meanwhile, the wealthy elite and corporations continue to obtain special tax breaks from Congress, which further undermines the revenue
base to fund social programs.

A Radical Program to End Inequality

The federal welfare reform program is doomed to fail. Not only will
poverty increase, but those living in states with mean-spirited social
policies will experience it most severely. As workers and middle-class
people continue to be ignored and disaffected by the political system,
state and local politicians will continue to hack away at the social
safety net. Unchallenged by any threat from either workers or the poor,
welfare benefits no longer need to serve the system's need to quell
social discontent or legitimate an increasingly inequitable economic
system. While AFDC payments and other welfare programs grew after
the urban unrest of the 1960s, the current absence of political pressure
from the poor and disenfranchised will allow the state to continue to
ignore their demands and needs. Meanwhile, following the passage of
their welfare reform agenda, corporate interests and their representatives in Congress are now free to go after "middle-class" entitlements
such as Social Security, education subsidies, veterans' benefits, and a
host of other programs that benefit the non-indigent and non-rich.

What can be done to stanch these reactionary social welfare policies
and bring about a more equitable distribution of wealth? In the short
run, it is crucial that the bottom 90 percent of income earners realize
that they must band together with the poor and mobilize around a new
political agenda that puts their economic interests ahead of those of the
rich. Such action also requires a new political party that can nullify
capital's dominance of the current political system. Second, there must
be a radical renovation of the tax structure such that taxes on inheri-
tances above about a million dollars would become confiscatory.

Third, only *earned* income below a certain threshold, perhaps $35,000, would be free from all taxes. Also, *all* income—from whatever source—would be subject to Social Security taxes. This would allow for a dramatic decline in the payroll tax rate for all workers and insure permanent solvency of the Social Security system. Fourth, social welfare programs would be designed to help families in the most direct manner possible: the government would pay parents to stay home (if they choose) to raise their children. The Scandinavian countries and other western European nations offer similar benefits to parents irrespective of income. Furthermore, since economists agree that goods and services produced at home are non-monetary forms of value, such a program would actually have the effect of raising the nation's gross domestic product. Finally, the federal government must get directly involved in providing employment opportunities to the poor and indigent that will be both meaningful and productive *and* pay a living wage. Given the numerous tasks that remain unmet or poorly provided by the free market—such as child and elder care, health care, new infrastructure, pollution reduction and cleanup, along with many other needed goods and services—the federal government will find ample demand for the labor now in their employ.

All of these steps, even though they fall short of the goal of public ownership of capital, would still be unacceptable to the leaders and defenders of the capitalist system. However, the system's failure, indeed its inability, to achieve and sustain some equitable measure of income distribution, along with its chronic problems of joblessness, discrimination, and poor economic growth, must eventually erode popular acceptance of existing arrangements. To be sure, the American dream of equal and unlimited opportunity for everyone has remained a powerful myth promoted by corporate propaganda, and it always has constrained the emergence of a truly Radical political and social movement in the United States. However, as the conflict between the dream and everyday reality sharpens, Radical alternatives to conventional social and economic measures will become matters of public debate and discussion. Just as America has used the promise of equal opportunity as the social glue to hold the nation together, the actual drift toward greater inequality becomes the device that undoes the entire production-for-profit system.

Financing Government

What Is a Fair System of Taxation?

In the most advanced countries, the following will be pretty generally applicable: . . . A heavy progressive or graduated income tax.

Karl Marx, The Communist Manifesto, *1848*

The flat tax is a deeply moral system. Purchase of tax privileges through political influence would end. We accept this social contract: a single tax rate and *no* tax breaks beyond the personal exemption. We will not try to increase government at someone else's expense. Every taxpayer will have to contribute.

William Poole, 1996

The current income tax system is often characterized as complex. A large part of the complexity results from eight decades of statutory and administrative modifications to address economic situations unforeseen when the income tax was originally enacted. . . . The Administration recognizes that the current tax system has some real and perceived problems.

Economic Report of the President, 1996

The Problem

Presently, the various governmental units of the United States—federal, state, and local—collect over $2 trillion in revenue from a lengthy and varied list of taxes. That's a "2" followed by *twelve* zeros. By any standard we are talking about "serious bucks." To put it in some perspective, the current annual tax bill of Americans is equal to about one-third of the nation's GDP (the annual dollar value of all new goods and services produced within our national borders). Indeed, the size of the national tax bill may prompt some readers to wonder if a more appropriate focus on an issue examining government financing might not be "Are Taxes Too High?" Alas, this is a bit off the target we are aiming at in this Issue. As we hope will be evident, "What Is a Fair System of Taxation?" is in most respects more important than the size of tax collections, and, at any rate, it is intricately tied to the question of size anyway.

The American passion for fairness in matters of taxation is a well-established historical fact. Indeed, the very birth of the nation is traceable to this outlook. "Taxation Without Representation," an eminently unfair idea from the perspective of many colonists, led some to hold a "tea party" in Boston Harbor in 1774 that directly defied the authority of the British colonial administrators. That spark soon fanned into the flame of the American Revolution and, eventually, the birth of the United States of America.

At least through most of the nineteenth century—with the probable exception of the Civil War era (1861–1865)—the individualistic and anti-central government temperament of most Americans meant a close eye was kept on the size of the federal government. Indeed, as late as 1902, the federal government's total spending amounted to only $485 million, or about one-third of all governmental outlays in the United States. Reflecting the outlook of Americans toward government in general, local government accounted for nearly 60 percent of all government spending. In any case, government spending of all kinds was equal to about 7 percent of the nation's GDP.

Alas, the twentieth century was to prove to be another matter altogether. Two major wars and an emerging redefinition of "appropriate" government responsibilities in the economy and social life of the nation not only ballooned the size of governmental outlays in general, but exploded the federal share to nearly two-thirds of total outlays. Such a spending explosion also required a commensurate increase in revenue sources to finance it. Throughout most of the prior century (with the exception of the Civil War years), most federal revenue was obtained from tariffs on goods entering the nation and from sales of public land. Federal taxes, in the sense we understand them today, were small and inconsequential. That would all change, however, as a growing federal government looked out for new revenue sources and ever so deliberately turned to personal income taxes, corporate income taxes, estate and gift taxes, and, finally, payroll taxes as sources for financing ever-expanding outlays.

The development of a federal income tax system occurred relatively late in our nation's history and not before a great deal of debate and controversy. For example, while the federal government had imposed an income tax to finance the Civil War, its constitutionality was challenged, but ultimately upheld by the Supreme Court in 1872. On the other hand, the Supreme Court reversed itself when it overturned portions of the federal income tax law of 1894. It was not until 1913—with the enactment of the Sixteenth amendment—that Congress actually acquired the "power to lay and collect taxes on incomes, from whatever source derived, without apportionment among the several states, without regard to any census or enumeration." The requirements of apportionment and enumeration had restricted the federal government to the option of imposing head taxes—which would have limited the capacity to raise revenue and introduced difficult issues about fairness.

When a federal income tax was initially levied, the personal exemption was quite generous, such that people earning below $4,000 (about $27,000 in 1998 dollars) did not pay any tax. Beyond incomes of $4,000, the federal income tax was mildly progressive, with tax rates rising in increments of less than 1 percent on those with incomes between $4,000 and $15,000 to a 6 percent rate on all income over $1 million. With family income averaging less than $2,000 in 1913, few Americans, even before exemptions and deductions were considered, saw the new income tax as much of a threat. Only 357,000 Americans filed

Table 7.1

Marginal Federal Income Tax Rates on Taxable Income for Selected Years

| | Income class | | | | | |
Year	$1,000	$5,000	$15,000	$50,000	$100,000	$1,000,000
1913	—	0.4%	0.8%	1.5%	2.5%	6.0%
1919	—	4.8	11.9	22.3	35.2	70.3
1929	—	0.3	1.9	8.5	14.9	23.1
1934	—	2.8	7.6	17.4	30.2	57.1
1944	11.5%	22.1	32.9	55.9	69.9	90.0
1951	8.2	19.3	30.2	53.5	67.3	87.2
1962	8.0	18.9	29.7	52.8	66.8	87.0

Source: "Historical Statistics, Series Y," pp. 319–332 as cited by Albert W. Niemi in *U.S. Economic History* (Chicago: Rand McNally Company, 1975), 121.

federal income tax returns for 1914. Over the next forty years, however, much was to change. A summary of effective tax rates for income groups, as shown in Table 7.1 exhibits the transformation in the federal income tax structure: Lower levels of income became increasingly subject to a tax liability. Tax rates rose for all levels of income, and they rose quite sharply for higher income levels.

During World War II, the government instituted automatic payroll deductions for federal taxes using a "graduated" schedule by which the tax rate rose with income. At that time, the government also reduced the personal exemption, which had the effect of widening the tax base to include middle- and lower-income classes. "Marginal tax rates"—or the rate applied to successively greater slabs of earned income—remained relatively high throughout the 1950s. With rising incomes and low inflation during these years, most Americans accepted the "ability to pay" principle of taxation. Under this approach, those with higher incomes would be taxed at a higher rate. In reality, however, because of the availability of numerous tax deductions and legal loopholes, few wealthy Americans ever paid the then-existing top statutory rate of 91 percent.

The first major change to the federal income tax structure was undertaken by John F. Kennedy, following his election in

1960. Faced with a sluggish economy, President Kennedy was counseled by his economic advisors to jump-start macroeconomic growth by lowering income tax rates and granting investment tax credits to the private sector. Although initially reluctant, the astute politician Kennedy realized that by tinkering with the tax system he could increase his popularity with both voters and the business community. While some Kennedy advisors believed that manipulating fiscal spending policies rather than taxes was a more effective and equitable means of managing the economy, more conservative advocates of tax cutting prevailed.

The federal income tax system did not change a great deal through the rest of the 1960s and 1970s. Following Kennedy's proposed reduction of the top marginal rate from 91 percent to 70 percent, which was enacted in 1964, not much changed for the average taxpayer. It was not until the early 1980s, following the election of Ronald Reagan, that Congress significantly altered the federal income tax system. First, the Economic Recovery Act of 1982 cut the top rate from 70 percent to about 50 percent. Second, the number of tax brackets was dramatically reduced, and third, many tax loopholes were supposedly closed. Although cutting taxes was claimed to reduce the federal budget deficit, by the mid-1980s it became clear that this was not going to happen. Nonetheless, another round of rate changes was undertaken with the Tax Reform Act of 1986, simplifying rate structure to two basic rates of 15 and 28 percent with the provision that the rate went to about 33 percent for high-income taxpayers. Throughout the rest of the decade and into the early part of the 1990s the federal tax code was changed in ways that adversely affected particular sectors—especially commercial real estate—and generally raised tax liabilities for the upper fifth of all taxpayers.

While the federal tax system remains essentially progressive, state and local governments typically use proportional and regressive taxes. A proportional or "flat" tax is one that takes a *constant* percentage of income. For example, Pennsylvania has a proportional state income tax. A regressive tax is one that takes a *declining* share of taxpayer income as income rises. Retail sales taxes are regressive because they are mostly levied on consumption items, which tends to claim a larger share of a poor person's total income compared to a wealthy individual. User and registration fees, excise taxes (especially on gasoline), filing fees, and other types of lump-sum payments are all examples of taxes that are effectively regressive. It can also be argued that federal employment taxes, such as Social Security contributions, are regressive because they are applied to wages and salaries under about $70,000. Income above this threshold, plus all unearned income (e.g., from dividends, interest, rents) is not subject to the Social Security tax.

In contrast, progressive taxes, as we have seen in the case of the federal income tax, take an *increasing* share of income from higher-income classes. The federal income tax is progressive in that higher tax rates apply to higher income. For example, in 1997 there were five different rates that applied to a single taxpayer: 15 percent on income up to $24,650; 28 percent on the next dollar up to $59,750; 31 percent on the next dollar up to $124,650; 36 percent on the next dollar up to $271,050; and 39.6 percent on each dollar of income greater than $271,050.

It is obvious that the type of revenue system a government chooses to employ—regressive, proportional, or progressive—necessarily says a lot about its sense of "fairness." Historically, the federal income tax system has been based on an "ability to pay" principle—the higher your earnings, the greater is your share of total taxes. However, over the last two decades, concerns about slowing productivity and declining living standards have introduced a new standard for viewing taxation. In particular, they have prompted a change in tax policy in an attempt to encourage savings and investment. Conservative "supply side" economists believed that reducing the top tax rates, as well as the number of income tax brackets, would cause wealthier individuals to increase their savings, which would spur capital formation and entrepreneurship. Simultaneously, lower tax rates would stimulate people to work harder and firms to invest in new plants and equipment and hire more workers. With more people working, tax collections would rise from enlarged payrolls, the federal deficit would decline, and overall economic growth would accelerate.

Before we join the debate over the merits of supply-side tax policies or any other perspective, Table 7.2 provides a cursory look at the source of federal tax receipts over the last half-century.

Table 7.2

Federal Government Receipts—1950, 1970, and 1990

	1950	1970	1990
Personal income taxes	35.9%	47.4%	44.3%
Corporate income taxes	34.1	15.7	10.0
Indirect business taxes	17.7	9.8	5.5
Contributions for Social Insurance	12.5	27.1	40.2
Total*	100.0%	100.0%	100.0%

Source: U.S. Department of Commerce, National Income and Product Accounts.
*Figures may not add due to rounding.

These figures clearly indicate the growing importance of personal income taxes and contributions for social insurance made by both wage earners and businesses as sources for federal receipts. On the other hand, both direct corporate income taxes and indirect business taxes have declined to about one-third of their respective shares in 1950. This shift in the federal tax base will figure prominently in the debate that follows.

Synopsis

Conservatives generally favor levies on consumption or other activities that will not distort an individual's decision to work or save. On the other hand, Liberals assert that since the level of income and wealth best reflects a person's ability to pay for governmental functions, a proportional or graduated income tax is the fairest system of taxation. Radicals argue that the long-term increase in the share of income borne by wage earners directly reflects the power of business elites to purchase congressional votes to ensure the passage of laws that will lower their share of the tax burden.

Anticipating the Arguments

- Why do Conservatives argue against progressive taxes as a means of financing government?
- What reasoning is employed by Liberals to justify progressive taxes as equitable?

- Why do Radicals advocate a steeply progressive tax on all sources of income?

THE CONSERVATIVE ARGUMENT

Ever since the economist Adam Smith specified the role for *limited* government interference in a market economy, most Conservative economists have recognized the need for a *small* public sector. However, the government sector in most advanced capitalist societies has expanded well beyond what Smith ever expected. To Smith, the state should provide for the national defense, educate citizens, administer justice, pay for "public works and institutions for facilitating the commerce of society," sustain the indigent, old, and infirm, and "support the dignity of the sovereign." Furthermore, government should pay for its provision and administration of goods and services by imposing taxes in an *equitable* and *consistent* manner. Thus, the overall goal of government tax policy should be to: (1) devise a system that is fair to all citizens and (2) help stimulate market forces that promote growth and capital formation.

Since the adoption of the federal income tax in 1913, the U.S. tax system has failed to adhere to these two basic principles. Instead, the income tax has been used to redistribute income from productive, hard-working taxpayers and businesses to government programs that support unproductive economic activities or unprofitable ventures. Moreover, onerous redistributive income taxes encourage individuals to avoid paying taxes by either working "off the books" or by seeking employment in the underground economy. The current tax system undermines the work ethic by significantly lowering after-tax wages. This causes workers to reduce their supply of labor to the market, often to the point where they choose to avoid work altogether and become dependent upon government welfare. Finally, the design and enforcement of the tax code is unnecessarily bureaucratic and intrusive, and imposes high costs of compliance.

Rather than adhering to Smith's maxim of an "equitable, certain, convenient and efficient" system of taxation, the U.S. government continues to confiscate an increasing share of taxpayers' incomes. Progressive income tax systems are based on the fallacious assumption that "wealthy" individuals do not gain as much satisfaction from an extra dollar of earnings as do those with lower incomes. Therefore, the government erroneously believes that it is actually improving society's well-being when it taxes away a "hardly missed" dollar from a high-income person and spends it on public goods or redistributes it to the lower end of the income distribution.

Little regard is given to the central role played by the savings and investments of thrifty individuals who provide the funds that ultimately drive growth and job creation. Moreover, since the poor tend to consume all their income, free markets crucially depend upon society's net savers to fund the enterprises (and some government activities) that put people to work. By taxing investors, the government only encourages savers to consume their surplus earnings, invest overseas, seek out unproductive "tax shelters," or engage in other tax-avoiding activities.

The Savings Crisis

Adam Smith was one of the first economists to understand that capitalism cannot thrive without the accumulation of a financial surplus for investment. The U.S. economy's ability to provide gainful employment and adequate income for all able-bodied workers is fundamentally determined by its savings rate. American capital markets must be able to harness the surplus funds of households, corporations, and foreigners and deploy them to the private sector for the purchase of new plants, property, and equipment. Thus, it is clear that without savings, the capital stock cannot expand and labor productivity cannot rise, which will ultimately result in a lower overall standard of living.

Unfortunately, the savings rate in the United States has been falling since about 1970. The decline in the personal savings rate is illustrated in Figure 7.1. In 1997, the savings rate was 3.8 percent—barely half its average value of 6.8 percent between 1950 and 1970.

The long-term consequences have been unambiguous: A decline in the savings rate has choked off domestic capital formation, which has led to a decline in overall labor productivity and thus a downfall in both income and mobility for numerous working people. In contrast, countries with much higher rates of internal savings—such as Japan and Germany—have had higher rates of investment, productivity, and real per capita income growth. It is abundantly clear that economies that cannot sustain an adequate rate of capital accumulation are destined to decline. Moreover, with heightened global competition for limited financial resources, new demands for investment capital can be expected to drain the savings of foreigners (who currently provide

Figure 7.1. **Personal Saving as Percent of Disposable Income**

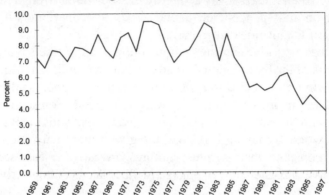

Source: Data from the Department of Commerce, Bureau of Economic Analysis.

about one-third of our domestic savings) from the American economy. Given these dire trends and circumstances, it is essential that federal tax policies be designed to increase capital formation by eliminating taxes on all forms of savings.

The Failure of Progressive Income Taxes

The legacy of progressive taxation has not been good. Since the early 1960s when the top marginal tax rate was over 90 percent, both the savings rate and labor productivity have steadily deteriorated while the share of taxes raised from personal income has steadily increased. Efforts to reverse this trend were helped with the passage in 1981 of President Reagan's tax reforms, which were designed to increase federal tax revenues by reducing the top marginal tax rates and by simplifying the federal tax code. The success of supply-side economics is supported by the fact that federal revenues increased by almost 50 percent from 1982 to 1988. While Ronald Reagan's tax policies generated higher revenues, the savings rate has continued to languish because Congress subsequently raised tax rates on the highest-income groups and steadfastly refuses to eliminate taxes on capital gains.

Although Liberals claim that the progressive income tax system helps to reduce income inequality in America, both disparities between income classes and the overall poverty rate have steadily increased since the early 1970s. This is because our tax laws stifle personal initiative by penalizing those who seek to better themselves. At its core, the current tax system only benefits the very poor—who are exempt from paying taxes—or the very rich who have already amassed their fortunes. For example, a graduated income tax often discourages risk-taking by reducing an entrepreneur's net return. This in turn chokes off innovation and competition while acting as a powerful deterrent to others who have the capacity to undertake new business ventures, but choose not to, for fear of seeing the fruits of their labor taxed away by the state. Furthermore, wealthy individuals living off a flow of unearned income will avoid risky investments in order to cover their ever-increasing tax liability.

Finally, the progressive income tax system is particularly onerous for families with two wage earners. When considered individually, a working husband and wife might not make very much money. However, when their incomes are combined, they are quickly pushed into the highest income tax bracket. In the case where one spouse earns most of the household's income, the less-compensated husband or wife often pays over half their income in taxes. Put simply, the current tax system is undermining the free market system by creating powerful disincentives to either work, save, or invest.

The Solution—A Progressive Consumption Tax

The Conservative argument for a progressive consumption tax is embedded in the notion that the economy remains fundamentally constrained by insufficient savings on the part of individuals. Moreover, an intrusive and overly complex federal tax system has created perverse incentives that diminish or misdirect investment activities, lowering productivity and encouraging profligate consumption. A progressive consumption tax would simultaneously address issues related to fairness and consistency that plague the current tax system.

Under a progressive consumption tax system, taxpayers would be allowed to deduct *all* funds that are saved or invested from their gross income. Money borrowed or taken out of savings would be included in taxable consumption. Since consumption is defined as income minus savings, computing an individual's tax liability from his or her paycheck would be a relatively straightforward process. There would be no need for investment tax credits or a capital gains tax since the government would allow a single, comprehensive "loophole" for all earnings not consumed—no matter what the source of those funds. Lobbyists would be banished from the halls of Congress because there could be no gain from trying to get special tax breaks for specific kinds of investments or business activities. Complicated tax formulas to account for inflation, depreciation, and a host of other problems related to capital accounting would be eliminated, since all income from savings and investments would be treated exactly the same—they would *all* be exempt from taxes.

Fairness would improve because tax rates on consumption would increase with higher levels of consumption. This would capture more government revenue from conspicuous and profligate consumption by wealthy individuals. Less affluent taxpayers would have more of an incentive to save because (1) there would be a lower tax rate on the last dollar consumed, and (2) they would gain the benefit of tax-exempt interest earnings. Business people would find it much easier to start new firms because all investments would be made in a tax-free environment. With a greater supply of savings forthcoming, the cost of capital would decline, and riskier and more innovative investment projects would be undertaken. Companies would be much more willing to start up new ventures and/or expand existing operations, thus leading to the hiring of more workers and an overall increase in output, income, and employment.

THE LIBERAL ARGUMENT

Political ideologues of either the right or left will eventually come to understand that an "optimal" system of taxation can never be achieved. Neither a program of "soaking the rich" nor one that primarily taxes consumption can ensure that the collective responsibilities we entrust to government will be funded. Economists have learned that there is no single tax system that can simultaneously achieve an equitable distribution of income, stable growth, high productivity, low unemployment and a myriad of other policy goals. While economic theories may purport to "prove" the superiority of a particular tax structure, tax systems—like all governmental undertakings—are *political* institutions that embody social and other noneconomic considerations. This fact cannot be evaded.

Most people would agree that the strength of the U.S. economy and society is largely due to the heterogeneous and pluralist nature of its population. This diversity enables individuals who possess a broad range of talents and abilities to harness America's resources for the betterment of all. However, wealth and skill are not evenly distributed throughout society, so that every individual cannot be expected to succeed solely on his or her initiative and skill. Nor is the private sector capable of insuring society's citizens against uncertainty and calamities of various sorts. Thus, an advanced capitalist economy requires its citizens to pool resources via government in order to offset and ameliorate income and job losses arising from recessions, foreign competition, technological unemployment, disease, natural catastrophes, and a host of other accidental and unforeseen factors. Put simply, the state must find a pragmatic method to raise money in order to undertake the necessary expenditures and projects required to hold a free market society together. The primary problem is to decide how best to obtain the funds needed for the provision of public goods and services.

While Adam Smith was correct in calling for the equitable taxation of those with roughly equal means, the question of how to tax *disparate* incomes is a more vexing issue. For example, a poor taxpayer and a rich taxpayer both receive the same amount of protection from the provision of defense services by the armed forces. Nevertheless, the question remains: Should the wealthy person still pay more for national defense because they have more to lose in the event of social unrest, war, or invasion? Alternatively, if a poor person lives in an area with a higher crime rate, should their tax liability be higher to pay for increased police protection? Even if we acknowledge differential abilities to pay, apportioning the appropriate benefits and costs to particular taxpayers cannot be guided by some fixed rule or principle.

Despite these ambiguities, it is quite evident that government revenues should be acquired in such a way as to maximize tax compliance and minimize avoidance and administrative costs. The development of both an efficient and an equitable system of tax collection should be the prime concern of lawmakers, even though the federal income tax system has grown in scope and complexity since its inception in 1913. While tax simplification would likely increase compliance with current tax statutes, the government could also significantly increase its revenues—without raising taxes—if it simply collected all that it was owed. In 1993, the IRS estimated a "tax gap" equal to about $150 billion, a figure then equal to three-fifths of the federal budget deficit. The problem has also been compounded by the persistence of many tax loopholes despite recent tax reform measures to close them. More-over, continued inequities in the incidence and distribution of many state and local taxes have heightened taxpayer frustration.

Nevertheless, the primary justification for the federal income tax rests mainly upon equity considerations. That is, a taxpayer's income is the best indicator of his or her ability to pay for the costs of govern-ment. On the other hand, those who are below some minimum income level can be easily excused from paying income taxes. In a similar vein, only the income tax is flexible enough to adjust an individual's personal circumstances to their tax liability. For example, suppose a family incurs substantial medical bills or loses a house to a fire or storm in a given tax year. In the first case, because the family "con-sumed" a substantial portion of their discretionary income in the form of medical goods and services, that family would now have a substan-tial tax liability. Moreover, replacing a home or car lost in a fire or accident would also subject a person to substantial consumption taxes. Finally, while many grumble about paying taxes each April 15, taxes fund many activities with significant benefits to all, including police and fire protection, schools, hospitals, sports stadiums, and museums.

The Success of the Progressive Income Tax

While few would dispute the complexity of our federal tax system, it has in fact accomplished its main task of raising government revenues in a generally equitable and efficient manner. Contrary to what Con-servatives claim, the top marginal tax rate is one of the lowest among the industrialized nations. Indeed, these same "overtaxed" nations have for the most part reported greater long-term efficiency and growth compared to the United States, thus disposing of the Conservative charge that our "soak the rich" tax strategy is a major cause of our recent sluggish economic performance. We should also remember that we pay taxes other than federal income taxes; for instance, state and local sales taxes, income, property, and use taxes. And, of course, corporate income and other business taxes are to some extent pushed onto consumers in the form of higher prices. When the effects of all of these taxes (many of which are highly regressive) are considered, the alleged "burden" of our progressive tax system is just not true.

What is true, however, is that our federal income tax system has been quite successful in distributing the tax burden: Those with higher incomes *do* pay a greater share of federal income taxes. In 1991, for example, just over two-thirds of the burden for personal income taxes were borne by those earning above $50,000 while those with incomes exceeding $75,000 paid for almost half of the total. In fact, a key reason why President Clinton was able to achieve a balanced federal budget—without slowing the economy—was that the progressive tax structure permits a slight tax increase on those with high incomes to generate a greater than proportional rise in tax revenues. Although some economists claim that taxes distort an individual's choice to work, consume, or invest, the evidence suggests that only very high marginal income tax rates actually discourage such behavior. Doctors, lawyers, accountants, and stockbrokers continue to supply just as many hours to the market, irrespective of any tinkerings that Congress might undertake with regard to the federal income tax law.

A progressive personal income tax also acts as a built-in stabilizer for the overall economy. During business expansions, it allows the government to collect relatively more revenues as output and incomes expand and proportionately less during recessions. Ronald Reagan used tax cuts to stimulate the economy during the 1981–82 recession. Unfortunately, the federal deficit exploded because he did not raise taxes on upper-income individuals, nor cut defense expenditures. Nevertheless, fiscal and tax policies—when applied in a reasonable and judicious manner—can be an effective means to maintain a stable balance between the growth of savings and income. While the current federal income tax system is far from perfect, it is clear that it satisfies the range of goals demanded by society.

THE RADICAL ARGUMENT

The development and workings of the American tax system must be understood in the context of its impact on wage earners as opposed to those who obtain their livelihood from "unearned" income in the form of profits, rents, interest, and dividends. Since the inception of the federal income tax on personal income in the early part of this century, most economists agree that wage earners have increasingly borne a higher share of the national tax burden. Given this trend, mainstream economists either argue for tax simplification—via a single tax rate—or emphasize the need to strengthen tax collection efforts at all levels of government. Alternatively, Radicals analyze the question of a fair tax system by whose interests are being served. For example, lucrative tax credits and esoteric tax deductions were not designed for wage earners who file the standard "E-Z" tax form. Rather, our complicated federal tax system and attendant tax laws directly reflect the efforts on the part of rich people, corporations and other monied interests to reduce their tax burden. The fact that the federal tax liability of capital has steadily *declined* for the last forty years only underscores the success of the richest 1 percent of income earners in shifting the costs of government onto the backs of the vast majority of working people.

Taxes and Accumulation

It has become an unquestioned premise of mainstream economic analysis that savings is the primary determinant of growth and accumulation. According to the Conservative paradigm, government attempts at taxing savings necessarily imply less growth in output, employment, and income. In addition, when the state runs a deficit, it not only has to raise taxes in the future, but in the short term it increases the overall cost of capital by bidding up interest rates to attract savings that would normally be allocated to private capital markets.

The logic of the Conservative argument suggests a strong inverse correlation between the top tax rate and the share of income devoted by an economy to investment. However, the most successful advanced capitalist economies exhibit a *positive* relation between taxation and investment. Figure 7.2 Panel A is a plot of the top income tax rate against the share of gross domestic product devoted to investment in machinery and equipment for eighteen advanced industrial economies that belong to the Organization for Economic Cooperation and Development (OECD). In addition, high-tax economies had both higher rates of investment in machinery and equipment and higher average savings rates (Figure 7.2 Panel B). Although this evidence does not make the case for higher taxes to stimulate investment, it does directly challenge the Conservative assertion that progressive taxes inhibit economic activity.

The bleating of the "overtaxed rich" belies reality, and their seemingly contradictory tolerance for government taxes to fund expenditures for warfare over those to enhance human welfare and dignity cannot be ignored. The federal income tax system initially taxed capital and upper-income individuals, while granting generous exemptions

Figure 7.2 Panel A: **Top Tax Rates and Investment/GDP.** Panel B: **Top Tax Rates and Savings Rates.**

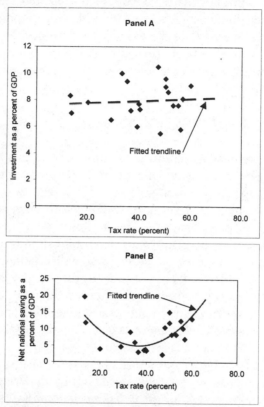

Source: Data from Organization for Economic Cooperation and Development.

to those further down the income ladder. The top marginal income tax rates have remained above the current top rate of 39.6 percent for most years since the inception of the federal personal income tax in 1913. However, since that time, personal exemptions for most taxpayers have been significantly reduced as has been the minimum income threshold where one begins paying taxes. Moreover, since 1935, funding the Social Security system has always been borne by workers whose earnings rarely exceed the salary ceiling beyond which no more payroll taxes are due ($68,400 for 1998). Thus, it is no surprise that the Social Security tax is the most highly regressive of all federal income taxes because it is capped at 6.2 percent of salaries up to about $68,400. For a person earning $100,000 the Social Security tax just over than 4.2 percent; at a salary above $200,000 the rate drops to about 2.1 percent. Finally, since about 1942, the federal government has reached further and further down the income distribution to find needed revenues. While the exigencies of World War II necessitated emergency taxes and debt financing, the government never returned to the prewar tax schedules that were much less onerous on working-class taxpayers.

The Problem with "Flat" Taxes

Since the passage of California's Proposition 13 in 1978, the "taxpayer revolt"—primarily against increased property taxes to fund municipal services, especially public schools—has spread to other states. Politicians at the national level have responded to taxpayer frustrations by proposing several changes to the current federal income tax system. Unfortunately, many plans to create a more simplified tax system also include many regressive features that will continue to foster an increase in the share of taxes borne by lower-income workers. There are currently several proposals in Congress to change the current federal income tax system. Most prominent among the Republican initiatives is a "progressive consumption tax." Let us briefly examine the problem with each of these tax schemes.

Presidents and lesser politicians have often enshrined their names in the history books not by noble deeds but by tinkering with the federal income tax code. The original federal income tax statute enacted in 1913 taxed unearned income (dividends, interest income, and the like) at a higher rate compared to earned (wage and salary) income. In contrast to the current climate favoring capital income, the first national tax scheme exempted almost all wage earners from federal taxes and permitted more generous personal exemptions. The top marginal personal income tax rate was first lowered by John F. Kennedy from 90 percent to 70 percent in 1964. Ronald Reagan lowered it to 50 percent in 1981 and even further to 33 percent in 1986. In addition to cutting the tax rates, lobbyists and other special interests have spent millions of dollars to induce Congress to include special rules that exempt particular businesses from federal taxes. Over the years, a vast and complicated system of tax laws and administrative rulings has created an unwieldy and highly inequitable tax system. The net result has been a decline in the share of federal taxes paid by large corporations and a notable increase in the tax burden of working people and small businesses.

The Conservative plan for a "progressive" consumption tax is a clever proposal to reconcile the inherent regressivity of consumption taxes with the current system, which taxes higher incomes at an increasing rate of taxation. To demonstrate its tenability, Conservatives appeal to the logic contained in the following mathematical example: Suppose an individual who makes $50,000 per year is taxed at a rate of 10 percent but also saves $5,000. A tax rate of 11.1 percent on an individual's consumption would be needed to raise the same amount of revenue because taxable income is reduced by the amount saved ($5,000). Though the example appears to be eminently reasonable, a problem arises as we move to higher incomes. Under current law, an individual taxpayer earning $10 million owes about $2.5 million in taxes (an average tax rate of 25 percent). Even if a very wealthy individual could consume $2.5 million of goods and services per year, the consumption tax rate would have to equal at least 100 percent to raise the same amount of revenue obtained from the current income tax structure. The point is that consumption tends to be a rather stable proportion of income for all individuals; however, wealthy people tend to consume a much smaller proportion of each dollar increment of income they earn. Short of forcing rich people to consume more, a consumption-based tax structure is inherently less burdensome for the wealthy compared to those with much less income.

A Return to Progressivity

In recent years, it has become quite unfashionable to argue for a tax system where the rate increases as an individual's income rises. Though Radical policy proposals are rarely put forward with any historical consistency or consensus, Marx and Engels argued for "a heavy progressive or graduated income tax" in their *Communist Manifesto* in 1848. Even Liberal economists have traditionally advocated a progressive income tax system based on the idea that an extra dollar of income for a middle-class or wealthy income earner provides diminishing satisfaction, and thus can be taxed at a higher rate compared to earnings below a mandated threshold. Adam Smith also believed that defense expenditures and education should be funded from "general contributions" and courts, roads, and other social infrastructure should be supported by tolls or fees. Smith also wrote in the *Wealth of Nations* that taxes should be levied in an equitable and consistent manner, *primarily* based upon an individual's ability to pay. Nevertheless, since about 1981, the progressivity of the federal income tax system has been reduced by cutting the top income tax rate while broadening the income range that applies to each rate. The net effect of these changes has been to significantly reduce the percent of taxes borne by the upper income groups.

While the federal income tax system has become less progressive, state and local tax schemes have also become less equitable. After the Reagan tax cuts of the early 1980s, many states simply adopted the federal tax brackets to their respective tax schedules. Furthermore, most local governments rely upon "regressive" property and sales taxes to fund most municipal activities. Property taxes are regressive because all incomes usually pay the same rate of tax but the property valuation of the poor, in contrast to the wealthy, is often above its actual market value. Meanwhile, sales taxes are inherently more burdensome to the poor because they tend to spend a higher portion of their income on taxable consumption items. Since property taxes are the major source of funding for public schools, it is obvious why richer communities always seem to have outstanding public school systems, irrespective of governmental tax policies and/or fluctuations in the general economy. Conversely, it is not surprising that poorer communities generally have inferior public schools, particularly when their communities are faced with permanent economic decline.

The Conservative desire for a consumption-based income tax system is part and parcel of their broader program to end all collectively funded social programs. In their view, an individual's ability for pecuniary gain should be the *sole determinant* of personal worth in society. Accordingly, any effort on the part of government to encumber private income is illegitimate and leads to a misallocation of scarce resources. It is only a short leap of Conservative logic to demonstrate how *any* income tax leads to the downfall of capitalism.

A Radical program for a more equitable tax system would start with a steeply progressive income tax system on *all* income. Those who earn less than a government-guaranteed income—say, $25,000 for a family of four—would automatically be exempt from all taxes. Second, most tax loopholes would be eliminated, inheritance taxes would be substantially increased, and a flat tax on all stock market transactions would be imposed. While long-term investors would not be taxed as heavily as short-term speculators, all capital gains would be subject to a highly progressive income tax structure. Under this tax system, no one would be prevented from accumulating wealth; however, it would not become the source of dynastic power for those who did not create it. Finally, all income—both earned and unearned—would be subject to a *progressive* Social Security tax. This would make the Social Security system solvent and eliminate all the inequities existing under current financing methods. For far too long, rich corporations and wealthy individuals have been able to use the political system to reduce their tax burden. It is time for the vast majority of Americans to direct their anger not so much at the tax collector, but at a Congress that is wholly incapable of creating a fair and equitable tax system. Ultimately, the vast majority of working-class Americans must band together to ensure that there will be an end to "taxation without representation."

Conclusion

Final Thoughts and Suggested Readings

Having reached the end of this volume of debates on contemporary economic issues, it is probable that the reader expects (perhaps even hopes for) the authors to make their pitches—to say straight out which of the representative paradigms is correct and which is not, perhaps each one to unveil his own grand program. Indeed, the opportunity is tempting. For an economist, it is practically a reflex to try to get in the last word, especially one's own last word. However, after much thought, we decided that such conclusions would spoil the entire effort. This book was undertaken to present the differing ideological alternatives as objectively as space and writing talents allowed so that the reader would be free to make personal choices on matters of economic policy.

We can hear some readers complaining: "Cop-out! You're avoiding presenting your own preferences and your own conclusions. You've taken the easy way out of the swamp." Not so. Delivering our own final polemics would in truth be ever so easy. But the book has been about questions and choices. The reader, then, shall be left in the uncomfortable position of making a choice among the paradigms and policy questions surveyed here. And that is the way it should be.

This perspective, however, must not be misunderstood. The authors have not intended to produce a "relativistic" conclusion in which any choice will do and one choice is as good as any other. The point is for the reader to make a *good* choice, and some policy choices *are* better than others. However, only a reasoned analysis of the facts and a critical study of the "truths" of this world will permit any of us to make wise choices.

The British economist Joan Robinson has said it best:

> Social life will always present mankind with a choice of evils. No metaphysical solution that can ever be formulated will seem satisfactory for long. The solutions offered by economists were no less delusory than those of the theologians that they displaced.
>
> All the same we must not abandon the hope that economics can make an advance towards science, or the faith that enlightenment is not useless. It is necessary to clear the decaying remnants of obsolete metaphysics out of the way before we can go forward.
>
> The first essential for economists, arguing amongst themselves, is to "very seriously," as Professor Popper says that natural scientists do, "try to avoid talking at cross purposes."*

Before we can "avoid talking at cross purposes" on economic matters, we must understand our fundamental differences in opinion and interpretation. Hopefully, this book has identified some of these important differences for the reader.

In undertaking this task, the authors were sorely tested. While trying to submerge our personal biases, we also had to master the biases of others. Perhaps we have not entirely succeeded on either count. Only the reader can judge. Nevertheless, such an endeavor has been extremely educational.

For readers who desire to dig deeper into economic ideologies and their application to contemporary issues, the following bibliography offers some landmark readings in the respective Conservative, Liberal, and Radical schools of economic thought.

Conservative

Banfield, Edward C. *The Unheavenly City.* Boston: Little, Brown, 1970.
Buckley, William. *Up from Liberalism.* New York: Honor Books, 1959.
Friedman, Milton. *Capitalism and Freedom.* Chicago: University of Chicago Press, 1962.
———. *Free to Choose.* New York: Harcourt Brace Jovanovich, 1980.
Gilder, George. *Wealth and Power.* New York: Basic Books, 1981.
Hazlitt, Henry. *The Failure of the "New Economics": An Analysis of the Keynesian Fallacies.* New York: Van Nostrand, 1959.

---

*Joan Robinson, *Economic Philosophy* (Garden City, NY: Anchor Books, 1964), pp. 147–148.

Kirk, Russell. *The Conservative Mind.* Chicago: Regnery, 1954.

Klamer, Arjo. *Conversations with Economists.* Totowa, NJ: Rowman and Allanhold, 1983.

Knight, Frank. *Freedom and Reform.* New York: Harper and Row, 1947.

Malabre, Alfred E., Jr. *Living Beyond Our Means.* New York: Vintage Books, 1987.

Marshall, Alfred. *Principles of Economics.* New York: Macmillan, 1890.

Rand, Ayn. *Capitalism: The Unknown Ideal.* New York: New American Library Signet Books, 1967.

Schumpeter, Joseph. *Capitalism, Socialism, and Democracy.* New York: Harper Brothers, 1942.

Simon, William E. *A Time for Action.* New York: Berkley, 1980.

Simons, Henry C. *A Positive Program for Laissez-Faire.* Chicago: University of Chicago Press, 1934.

Smith, Adam. *An Inquiry into the Nature and Causes of the Wealth of Nations,* 1776.

Stein, Herbert. *Presidential Economics: The Making of Economic Policy from Roosevelt to Reagan and Beyond.* New York: Simon and Schuster, 1985.

Von Hayek, Friedrich. *The Road to Serfdom.* Chicago: University of Chicago Press, 1944.

Von Mises, Ludwig. *Socialism: An Economic and Sociological Analysis.* New Haven: Yale University Press, 1959.

Liberal

Berle, Adolf A. *The Twentieth Century Capitalist Revolution.* New York: Harcourt Brace Jovanovich, 1954.

Clark, John M. *Alternative to Serfdom.* New York: Random House/Vintage Books, 1960.

———. *Social Control of Business.* New York: McGraw-Hill, 1939.

Friedman, Benjamin. *Day of Reckoning.* New York: Random House, 1988.

Galbraith, John Kenneth. *The New Industrial State.* Boston: Houghton Mifflin, 1967.

———. *The Affluent Society.* Boston: Houghton Mifflin, 1971.

———. *Economics and the Public Purpose.* Boston: Houghton Mifflin, 1973.

———. *Economics in Perspective.* Boston: Houghton Mifflin, 1987.

Hansen, Alvin. *The American Economy.* New York: McGraw-Hill, 1957.

Heilbroner, Robert. "The Future of Capitalism" in *The Limits of American Capitalism.* New York: Harper and Row, 1966.

———. *The Nature and Logic of Capitalism.* New York: Norton, 1985.

Heller, Walter W. *The Economy: Old Myths and New Realities.* New York: Norton, 1976.

Keynes, John M. *The General Theory of Employment, Interest, and Money.* New York: Harcourt Brace Jovanovich, 1936.

Lekachman, Robert. *The Age of Keynes.* New York: Random House, 1966.

Okun, Arthur M. *The Political Economy of Prosperity.* New York: Norton, 1970.

Reagan, Michael D. *The Managed Economy.* New York: Oxford University Press, 1963.

Reich, Robert B. *Tales of a New America.* New York: Times Books, 1987.
Shonfield, Andres. *Modern Capitalism: The Changing Balance of Public and Private Power.* New York: Oxford University Press, 1965.
Thurow, Lester C. *Dangerous Currents.* New York: Random House, 1983.
————. *The Zero-Sum Society.* New York: Basic Books, 1980.
————. *The Zero-Sum Solution.* New York: Simon and Schuster, 1985.

Radical

Baran, Paul. *The Political Economy of Growth.* New York: Monthly Review Press, 1957.
Baran, Paul, and Paul M. Sweezy. *Monopoly Capital.* New York: Monthly Review Press, 1966.
Botwinick, Howard. *Persistent Inequalities.* Princeton, NJ: Princeton University Press, 1993.
Bowles, Samuel, and Herbert Gintis. *Property, Community, and the Contradictions of Modern Social Thought.* New York: Basic Books, 1986.
Bowles, Samuel, and Richard Edwards. *Understanding Capitalism.* New York: Harper and Row, 1985.
Brouwer, Steve. *Sharing the Pie: A Citizen's Guide to Wealth and Power in America.* New York: Henry Holt and Company, 1998.
Domhoff, William. *Who Rules America?* Englewood Cliffs, NJ: Prentice-Hall, 1967.
Dowd, Douglas. *The Twisted Dream.* Cambridge, MA: Winthrop, 1974.
Duboff, Richard. *Accumulation and Capital.* Armonk, NY: M.E. Sharpe, 1990.
Franklin, Raymond S. *American Captialism: Two Visions.* New York: Random House, 1977.
Gordon, David M. *Fat and Mean.* New York: The Free Press, 1996.
Henwood, Doug. *Wall Street.* London: Verso, 1997.
Kolko, Gabriel. *Wealth and Power in America.* New York: Praeger, 1962.
Magdoff, Harry. *The Age of Imperialism.* New York: Monthly Review Press, 1967.
Mandel, Ernest. *Marxist Economic Theory.* New York: Monthly Review Press, 1967.
Marx, Karl. *Capital.* 1867.
O'Connor, James. *The Fiscal Crisis of the State.* New York: St. Martin's Press, 1973.
Robinson, Joan. *An Essay on Marxian Economics.* London: Macmillan, 1942.
Shaikh, Anward M., and E. Ahmet Tonak. *Measuring the Wealth of Nations.* Cambridge: Cambridge University Press, 1994.
Sherman, Howard. *Radical Political Economy.* New York: Basic Books, 1972.
————. *Stagflation: A Radical Theory of Unemployment and Inflation.* New York: Harper and Row, 1976.
Strachey, John. *The Nature of Capitalist Crisis.* New York: Covici, Friede, 1933.
————. *The Theory and Practice of Socialism.* New York: Random House, 1936.
Sweezy, Paul. *The Theory of Capitalist Development.* New York: Monthly Review Press, 1942.
Williams, William A. *The Great Evasion.* Chicago: Quadrangle Books, 1964.

Index

About The Authors

Robert B. Carson is professor emeritus with the Department of Economics and Business at the New York state university college at Oneonta. He pioneered the unique approach of teaching economics by addressing economic issues from the Conservative, Liberal, and Radical positions with the first edition of *Economic Issues Today* in 1978. He has authored twelve books on economics, including *What Economists Know* (1990), which has been reprinted abroad in Spanish, Portuguese, Russian, and Arabic editions. Dr. Carson is an expert on the public regulation of American railroads.

Wade L. Thomas is associate professor and chair of the Department of Economics and Business at the state university college at Oneonta. He has served as president and vice president of the New York State Economics Association, has published numerous journal articles, and is experienced in the use of educational technology and webpage creation. He coauthored *The American Economy: Contemporary Problems and Analysis* (1993) with Robert B. Carson.

Jason Hecht has been working as an economist in the property-liability insurance industry for the past sixteen years while also teaching as an adjunct faculty member at several New York City area colleges. He has published in both academic and business publications and also works as an independent consultant to the telecommunications and pharmaceutical industries. Dr. Hecht is currently an assistant professor of finance at Ramapo College of New Jersey.